Before You Go

What Every Parent Needs to Say and Every Kid Needs to Hear

Dr. William Rice

OUTCOME PUBLISHING

818 West Diversey Parkway, Suite W
Chicago, IL 60614

BEFORE YOU GO
What Every Parent Needs to Say and Every Kid Needs to Hear
by Dr. William Rice

Published by Outcome Publishing
818 West Diversey Parkway, Suite W
Chicago, IL 60614
www.outcomepublishing.com

First Edition

Printed in the United States of America

1. Religion: Spirituality General
2. Self-Help: Spiritual
3. Religion: Christian Life – Personal Growth

Dedication

To Amanda, Anna and Stephen. Of all the titles I have been given and honors I have received, there is none greater than being called "Dad." Every time I think of you, I smile.

Ross,
May you grow & lead with all wisdom,
Malachi 4:6

Acknowledgements

I am grateful to the people and staff of Calvary Church in Clearwater whose love for their pastor and greater love for the truth of God's word makes my work a continual joy.

Special thanks to Kelly White, gifted writer and member of our church, who carefully read through the manuscripts of this book and whose input and valuable suggestions made this book much better than it would have been without her help.

Endorsements

Pastor Willy Rice has opened his heart and allowed us to listen in as he escorts his own children into adulthood. "Before You Go" is a must read for every parent who wants to know how to share their deepest faith with their sons and daughters. And it's a must resource for every young man or woman who wants to begin their journey with a faith that will stand the test of time.

Barry Banther
Past President of Trinity College of Florida
Author of "A Leaders Gift
- How to earn the right to be followed"

"What if you as a parent or grandparent had the opportunity to have your son or daughter sit down with a famous General, a former President, a legendary coach or one of the wisest leaders in the world? If you are like me, you would rearrange your schedule and move every obstacle to provide your child with that kind of experience. My good friend William Rice in his excellent book "Before You Go....What Every Parent Needs to Say and Every Child Needs to Hear" provides the opportunity to have eight meals with Solomon - the wisest man to ever live. I've spent my life both through Student Leadership University and speaking at schools and universities trying to make an imprint on young people

before they go off to college. Written by a father, a leader, a shepherd, and a counselor, this book has captured the wisdom of Solomon with perfect relevance for today's cultural issues. This is a must read."

Dr. Jay Strack
President & Founder
Student Leadership University
Slulead.com

The toughest job in the world is being a parent. My friend Willy Rice has written a heart-warming book that will help both moms and dads be the kind of parents to paraphrase Luther "make your kids sorry to see you leave home and glad when you return." Read it, put it into practice and your kids will thank you!

Dr. James Merritt
Author and Lead Pastor
Cross Pointe Church, Duluth, Georgia

Dr. Rice has done every parent a huge favor by allowing us to listen to his letters to his own son who is leaving home to begin his university---and life-beyond-home---experience. I well remember the poignancy of the moment in my own life when our own son took that step. "Have I," I pondered, "told him everything he's going to need for the journey!" Dr. Rice's book is solid, readable, sane, pragmatic, and thoroughly biblical. A thesaurus of vital life-skills. An infallible spiritual GPS. A trustworthy moral compass. Do yourself and others a favor by reading, and re-reading it, and encouraging others---especially young men---to do the same.

Dr. Bill Anderson
Pastor Calvary Baptist Church
Clearwater, Florida (1975-2002)

I highly recommend William Rice's book on Proverbs. Proverbs has been described as Hebrew Bumper Stickers. They are sermons in a sentence that are ancient but timeless lessons that work in our advanced society. William's personal examples provide lessons that become powerful principles for today's family. Read this book carefully because it can be a life manual from ancient days that will become a resource for an awesome family.

Dr. Charles Lowery
Author, Speaker, Psychologist

William Rice has given every parent and every child a great gift. This book is Biblical, practical, and personal. It contains a wealth of wisdom that will enable young people to live godly, successful lives in a sinful world. And his eight major life lessons will benefit adults as well! If you are a parent or a grandparent, get this book and use it.

Dr. David Clarke
Christian Psychologist, Speaker
Author of 11 books, including –
I Don't Want a Divorce and The Top Ten Most Outrageous Couples of the Bible

Do you need a reliable navigational tool to help you prepare your children for their journey in life? In Before You Go, Willy Rice shares essential truths that parents need—truths to steer their children in the right direction and pave the way for a meaningful future."

Mark Merrill
President, Family First

Table of Contents

Introduction

It was early in the spring a few years back when it hit me: time is almost up. Like the overturned hourglass, I was watching the final grains of sand slip through. It was almost over.

Cheryl and I married young and were blessed with three children. Our first two, Amanda and Anna, were precious girls and our third, Stephen, a son. Like millions of parents before us, we had watched ours grow from infants into adolescents and then stride across a graduation stage and step into their future. We marveled at the passage of time and wondered where the years had gone.

By the time Stephen was preparing to graduate High School both our daughters were well on their way into adulthood. Our oldest had graduated college, married and was pregnant. Our second daughter was nearing the end of her college experience and now Stephen was about to leave as well. As any parent who has walked that path knows, it gives you pause. You think about the passage of time, the hastening of the pace and you wonder if you said the things that really needed to be said. Did we really teach all the lessons that needed to be taught? Have we adequately prepared them for the next step?

My ponderings took me back to the timeless truths of Proverbs. The book is after all the words from one generation to another. It is a collection of observations about life from one of the wisest men who ever lived. I noticed how the writer, Solomon, addressed his words to the next generation as he spoke often of "My Son." I saw some major themes in the book and began to organize the Proverbs into eight major categories of advice. I began to think about my son and indeed all the graduates who pass by every year and wondered if there might be some merit in sharing these truths along with my thoughts.

Out of that study grew these letters and this material. I found eight major lessons that every parent needs to speak and every kid needs to hear. I wanted to make sure I said what needed to be said before the hourglass ran empty. Out of that simple fatherly desire has come this book. Each chapter begins with a letter and focuses on one of the major themes from Proverbs. This book pulls together a collection of some of the very best Proverbs that distill essential wisdom that one generation needs to pass along to another. Most every parent knows there are some things that need to be said before it is too late. My prayer is that this book will help you say it. I've written as if I were speaking to the next generation, a high school graduate perhaps. If that's you, I invite you to listen to some practical wisdom passed down through the ages. I'll try not to get in the way. For the parents and grandparents reading this, I hope this book helps you say what you want to say and perhaps inspires you to write a few letters of your own.

It's not every day that you get to sit down with one of the world's smartest men to talk about life, but the book of Proverbs gives you that chance. So let's take a look at what one generation should say to the next. Let's look at what every parent needs to say and every kid needs to hear. One last time. Before you go.

Letter One

Wisdom:
Beware the Fork in the Road

❖

Dear Son,

We approach the end and a new beginning all at the same time. These are significant days. In just a few weeks you will walk across this very platform in a ceremony that marks a reality. You are graduating. You will take the next step. You will move on. To paraphrase Churchill, it is not the end, nor even the beginning of the end, but it is surely the end of the beginning for you. Practice is over. Game on.

Soon you will leave for a new place and a new challenge. College is a great time. And I've been wondering: Did I say the things that really matter? Have I conveyed the lessons along the way, the lessons that really make the difference between a life well lived or wasted? I do hope that as we rose up and sat down, as we walked and as we talked, as we laughed and as we played, that somewhere, somehow some portion of wisdom has passed into your hands.

I talk to plenty of people who would like to be 18 again. They would love a do-over on relationships, habits, choices, investments, words. But you only get to do it once. You only get to be 18 once. You only get to go to college once. You only get to do your 20's once and can live your life anyway you want to, but you only get to do it once. We won't pass this way again.

Some will define life as a series of circumstances beyond your control, or chances that just happen. They are partly right, but mostly wrong. There are many things that will happen over which you have no control. But life is mostly about the choices you will make. Most of your regrets will come from things you do to yourself and people you love. Most of your victories will come because you made the right decision that took you to the right path that led you to the right outcome. Choices do matter and none of that factors God out of the equation. As you will see it is His hand that will guide you to the right choice, the right outcome and His grace that enables you to find and embrace the right path.

So here you are: 18, graduating with the world in front of you. The road ahead contains many turns and many choices. Beware the fork in the road, for your choices will become your destiny. Fortunately for you there is a guide, a light for your steps and a lamp for your feet. Think of it as a GPS for life. There is wisdom that comes from those who have walked the paths you will walk. It comes from those who have already faced the same choices and challenges you will face. The context may change, the surroundings may appear new, but I assure you the choices are not, neither are the outcomes. They are predictable. Choose one path and you will end up in one place, choose another and the outcome changes. Beware the fork in the road for you are charting the course for your life. You are deciding your destiny.

So I thought I'd pass a few of these nuggets of wisdom along. What you do with them is up to you. I'll love you either way, but oh the blessings that will be yours if you follow the right guide. Here they are: lessons from the past. Truths that transcend time. A few lessons from the heavenly Father, the source of all truth, contained in the book of wisdom called Proverbs. Just some final lessons before you go.

Love,

Dad

Chapter One

Wisdom: Beware the Fork in the Road

Listen, my son, to your father's instruction and do not forsake your mother's teaching. They are a garland to grace your head and a chain to adorn your neck. My son, if sinful men entice you, do not give in to them.
(Proverbs 1:8-10)

Your Father has some advice. Whether you were blessed with an earthly father who desired to pass along wisdom or not, whether you came from a healthy family or an unhealthy one and regardless of where you are on the journey of life, you have a Heavenly Father and He has some advice to share. You have a Heavenly Father who has provided a lamp for your feet and a light for your path. You have a Heavenly Father who has some counsel to give you.

The Book of Proverbs is known as 'The Book of Wisdom' because it was written to show us how to live wisely. Solomon was known both in his day and in ours for his vast wisdom and towering intellect. In Proverbs he collects his observations about life and principles for living and succeeding with God and people. His target? The next generation. I'll prove it to you. In some of the very first verses he writes,

The proverbs of Solomon son of David, king of Israel:
For attaining wisdom and discipline; for
understanding words of insight;
(Proverbs 1:1-2)

Solomon is saying, "I want you to be wise," and then in verse four he reveals his target audience,

For giving prudence to the simple, knowledge and discretion to the young—
(Proverbs 1:4)

Who is he writing to? He is writing to those who are young. The main focus in the book of Proverbs is an older teenager, about to graduate, ready to take on life. One of the wisest men who ever lived was basically saying, *If I had one more message to give, I would give it to the graduating class. I would give it to those who are still young. I would tell them how to be wise.*

I started looking at this book with fresh eyes as my son, Stephen, was preparing to graduate from High School. I noticed that Proverbs is not only directed to the young, but that specifically Solomon seemed to be speaking to his son. In fact, forty-five times in this book the word 'son' is used, and twenty-three of those times (more than half) it is used as part of a command as in "my son, do this," or "my son, do that." Here are just a few of these verses.

My son, if you accept my words and store up my commands within you,
(Proverbs 2:1)

My son, do not forget my teaching,...
(Proverbs 3:1)

My son, do not despise the Lord's discipline...
(Proverbs 3:11)

Listen, my son, accept what I say, and the years of your life will be many.
(Proverbs 4:10)

My son, pay attention to my wisdom, listen well to my words of insight.
(Proverbs 5:1)

My son, keep your father's commands and do not forsake your mother's teaching.
(Proverbs 6:20)

My son, keep my words and store up my commands within you.
(Proverbs 7:1)

My son, if your heart is wise, then my heart will be glad; *(Proverbs 23:15)*

Listen, my son, and be wise, and keep your heart on the right path.
(Proverbs 23:19)

Be wise, my son, and bring joy to my heart;...
(Proverbs 27:11)

Now whether Solomon was addressing his own biological sons, or using the term "son" in a more general sense, he was surely addressing the next generation, both sons and daughters as well. He was saying, "I have something you should listen to, and the sooner you hear it, the better off you will be." You see, Solomon collected his observations about life and passed them along in a book of sayings so that we can grow wise.

This wisdom, lived out and passed on through generations, has the potential to leave God's mark on all of history, and transform your life in the process. If only you would decide to seek wisdom now.

In the Book of Proverbs, Solomon addresses nearly every topic imaginable: sex, money, communication, relationships, work, marriage, anger, character, honesty, parenting, and on and on the list goes. As I thought about Stephen's departure, I took time to read through Proverbs carefully and noticed eight major categories of teaching that every young person needs to learn. So I collected the Proverbs and grouped them into those eight categories, in an effort to distill down the essence of what Solomon had to say. I wanted my son to hear these enduring truths, delivered in a fresh way. As I wrote, I felt an urging to share them with others in our church, and then to pass them along to you in this book.

Maybe you are a student trying to make sense of your life and future, perhaps a graduating senior on the brink of adulthood. More than anything, I want you to hear these teachings about life from one of history's wisest men. Maybe you are a parent, a grandparent, or a friend of someone about to take an important step from adolescence to adulthood. Hopefully, this book will help you pass along some truth of your own. But then, who doesn't need to hear wisdom from above? No matter where you are on your journey through life, why not stop and take a fresh look at these lessons? You have a Father, a heavenly Father, and His wisdom is what we need most of all.

So let's start with the overall idea of wisdom. What exactly is it? Where does it come from? How do you get it? Solomon has a lot to say about the importance of gaining wisdom, starting in the very first chapter.

Listen, my son, to your father's instruction and do not forsake your mother's teaching. They will be a garland to grace your head and a chain to adorn your neck. My son, if sinners entice you, do not give in to them. (*Proverbs 1:8-10*)

When you talk about wisdom, the first thing most people think about is intelligence, or being exceptionally "smart." We look at a smart person and say, "That guy is really wise." But wisdom is not the same thing as knowledge. Knowledge is the ability to accumulate information, and that's a good thing, a wonderful gift. But wisdom, when reduced to its essence, is knowing how to make the right choices. Wisdom is standing at a fork in the road and knowing whether you should go to the left or to the right. That's wisdom. When you make enough right choices, you're wise. Wisdom is making those right choices again and again. It sounds simple, I know, but so many make the wrong choices.

Your Direction Becomes Your Destiny

I like trips. My family will tell you I like to plan. I enjoy both making the plan and executing it. My wife Cheryl takes joy in sitting back to watch the plan unfold. My family has input on the destination, but I get the trip together. I figure out where we're going to stay, what we're going to see, and how we're going to get there. Several years ago when our children were still young we planned our first-ever family trip to the Big Apple – New York City. Now, we weren't flying into JFK or LaGuardia and taking a cab downtown. No, the plan was to drive the minivan into the belly of the beast. We were headed into one of the largest and most exciting cities in the world and I was pumped. Armed with maps and a well-studied plan, I knew every bridge we were going to cross and had highlighted every turn. I had studied the one-way roads, the narrow roads and the back-roads. I knew how to get there. Long before the days where GPS systems sucked the challenge right out of the navigation experience, I was a man with a plan. I had booked a hotel in the center of Times Square to which we were going to drive up, hand the keys to the bellhop, and begin our adventure. This was going to be big, and we were ready.

The momentous day began just outside of Philadelphia, where we had stayed the night before. Actually, that's when the trouble began. Our hotel was just across the Jersey line, and was supposed to be one of those hotels situated right off of an exit. But when we wearily abandoned the interstate that night, it wasn't actually there. It was more like, "exit interstate, drive three miles, exit left, drive two miles and then you find it." Mildly frustrated, we finally arrived at our hotel. The next morning we woke up, loaded the minivan and resumed our adventure. Destination: New York City, in less than three hours. Look out, here comes the mini-van! But within seconds of pulling out of the hotel parking lot, we landed on some kind of toll road going who knows where. There was no option for a U-turn, and the road just kept going on and on. For a while I ignorantly assumed that the road would take us to the Interstate at some point, but that point never came. I started to get frustrated. "Why don't they have a sign?" I thought. "Why didn't someone tell us how to get to the interstate when we checked out?" The blood started to rise in my head, but I regained my composure at the sight of an exit sign. Veering off the interstate, I quickly realized I had just been dumped onto another toll road. The next thing I know, I'm heading in the wrong direction with the next closest exit miles away.

At this point, I'm beginning to lose it. We can't even get to the interstate! I'm lost and we haven't even gotten started. Here we've made it within three hours of the city that never sleeps and I'm ready to call it a day and go back to bed. I'm getting angrier by the second, royally blowing it with the kids, and they are getting really quiet. I mean *real* quiet. Come to think of it, they were probably hunkering on the floorboard thinking, *I know my dad is a pastor, but I'm not seeing much Jesus in him at this moment. If only all those church people could see him now.* Right about then, my wife decided to break the silence with a suggestion, a humiliating and deeply offensive suggestion. She said, "Why don't you stop and ask for directions?" Can you believe that? She had the nerve to call me out right in front of the kids! "No!" I lashed back, "I'm not going to stop and ask for anything! We have got to find the interstate." After a couple more turns, my determination turned to desperation. I came to realize that we were on a side road and completely lost (maybe those GPS things were a good idea after all). That was the last straw. I lost it, completely lost it. At this point, everyone was silent. I decided to pull into a small convenience store, reluctantly trying to accept the fact that I was going to have to ask for directions. I circled around the back of the store intending to pull around the building and park along the opposite side. Instead, I brought my minivan nose to nose with a dumpster. After all of the excitement and anticipation, I managed to drive my family down a one-way alley that ended at a garbage dumpster. I put the car in park, leaned my head on the steering wheel, and just sat there for a moment, seething. It was quiet, really quiet. No one was breathing. Finally, Cheryl decided to speak. She just couldn't help it. She asked, in a somewhat sarcastic tone, "Is this where you wanted to go?" No! That was not where I wanted to go! I didn't wake up that morning and think, "What I really want to do today is park in front of a garbage dumpster in New Jersey." Why did we end up there? Because that was the road I had chosen. And the road that you choose will determine your final destination, whether you like the destination or not. The same is true in life. The direction you choose becomes your destiny. It's really not that hard. It's not that complicated. Your direction becomes your destiny. You must choose wisely.

As a pastor, I meet with people every week whose lives are parked in front of a dumpster. Their marriage is in front of a dumpster. Their kids are in front of a dumpster. Their finances are in front of a dumpster. They write me letters or come to my office asking the same questions, "How did we end up here? How could God let this happen to me?" I see them weary and broken and my heart is heavy, and yet another part of me wants to say, "Really? You didn't see this coming? You lived beyond your means. You kept borrowing. You invested in multiple get-rich-quick schemes and are now in your forties wondering why your life is parked in front of a financial dumpster?" I see people who have lived outside of God's moral standard and yet they say, "How could God let this happen?" But the hard response is: "You want to blame that on God? You're the one who took the road. You're the one who chose the path, and the path you chose led to where you are. It's not God's fault." You see, maybe if they had learned about the fork in the road, they would have taken a different path. A different path would have led to a different outcome.

Here's the truth about life: The decisions you make become the direction you take, and the direction you take becomes the destiny you create. Did you catch that? The decisions I make, become the directions I take, and that turns into the destiny I create.

I know a family that checked out of church twenty years ago. They just checked out. They had other things to do, other pursuits. They had sports. They had money. They would tell you, "Oh we believe in God" but they just opted out of doing life with a body of believers. Now, twenty years later, their kids don't know God. They were left saying, "How could this happen?" They chose the path and the path they took led them to the dumpster. The decisions you make, become the direction you take, and it turns into the destiny you create. So Solomon writes a book, and he says, "Listen, you need to know something. Life is about the path you take."

Then you will understand what is right and just and fair—every good path.
(Proverbs 2:9)

Do not set foot on the path of the wicked or walk in the way of evil men.
(Proverbs 4:14)

The path of the righteous is like the first gleam of dawn, shining ever brighter till the full light of day.
(Proverbs 4:18)

Keep to a path far from a wicked woman...
(Proverbs 5:8)

In the way of righteousness there is life; along that path is immortality.
(Proverbs 12:28)

The path of life leads upward...
(Proverbs 15:24)

The man who strays from the path of understanding comes to rest in the company of the dead.
(Proverbs 21:16)

A man of integrity walks securely, but he who takes crooked paths will be found out.
(Proverbs 10:9)

In the paths of the wicked lie thorns and snares, but he who guards his soul stays from them.
(Proverbs 22:5)

These are only a few of the many proverbs instructing us about how the paths we choose ultimately impact our destiny. If you want to avoid the dumpster you had better gain wisdom. This is why Proverbs is a great book when you're eighty, but it is especially great when you're eighteen. At eighteen, there are still a lot of forks in the road in front of you. So here is the big question; *where do you find wisdom*? How do you know which road to take? It looks easy when you're peering into someone else's life, but it can be really foggy when you're staring down your own fork in the road. So where do you find wisdom? Solomon told us.

You find wisdom in God. The first place to find wisdom is in God.

The fear of the Lord is the beginning of knowledge,
but fools despise wisdom and discipline.

(Proverbs 1:7)

This verse is repeated several times in Proverbs because it is so important. The starting place for a life of wisdom lies in knowing God and acknowledging his supremacy over all things. It sounds something like, "Okay, God. You know what? I know I don't know everything. But you do!" The opposite of that is to think, "I am the ruler of my own destiny. I am in charge of my life. I must follow my heart and trust my gut." The truth is your heart and your gut will bring you to a dumpster in New Jersey if you're not careful, or maybe a lot worse. Jeremiah the prophet wrote, "The heart is deceitfully wicked…" We are warned over and over in Scripture not to follow our heart, but to follow God's heart. You can start by saying, "God, you are smarter than I am. You know where each road leads and I don't. I know you love me. So, would you help me choose the right path?"

> *It's the Lord who gives wisdom. From His mouth come knowledge and understanding."*
>
> *(Proverbs 2:6)*

The more things change, the more they stay the same. Just this week I noticed one example after another of people who made foolish choices. By the time you read this these particular stories will be old news, but I guarantee there will be fresh examples sitting on the newsstands. Why? People continue to make the same imprudent choices. They keep taking the same bad directions and ending up behind the same smelly dumpsters.

This week I read about a Division 1 football coach with an 18 million dollar salary contract over several years and a projected top five team. He was at the pinnacle of his career. Then suddenly he lost his job. Not because he wasn't a good coach, but because his own personal immoralities led to indiscretions and unethical behavior, and his university fired him.

Then I read about a professional athlete in my area that retired from the NFL. In his playing career he signed contracts valuing $80 million. In addition, he has a current job that pays him $540,000. That's not a bad gig, huh? Most of us would be happy to trade salaries with him. But this week, at the age of thirty-nine, he filed for bankruptcy. One would think that $80 million would at least get a guy into his forties, right?

Then I saw a third story about a major league manager at the top of his game. He gave an interview to a magazine and said something completely stupid and uncalled for. He infuriated the residents of his city and the fans of his ball club. When the league suspended him, many weren't satisfied and some even wanted him fired. Once again, the very same questions came to my mind, "How could he do that? How could he say that?" My head was spinning. In one week in the news, you've got a guy who can't control his sex drive, another guy who can't control his money, and yet another who can't control his mouth. It's the same stuff. The players change, the names change, the uniforms change and the situations change, but it's the same story.

You may be reading this at 16, 17 or 18 years of age and thinking, "It's a different world now," but it's not. Read the Book of Proverbs. The things that tripped people up and ruined their lives thousands of years ago are the very same things you will face. They are the same forks in the road, nothing new. You see, true wisdom knows not to trust its heart or its gut, but to trust God. True wisdom is found in Him, because He alone knows where the roads lead. "

Another place to gain wisdom is from *previous generations.* Look at what Solomon said in Proverbs 1:8:

> *Listen, my son, to your father's instruction and do not forsake your mother's teaching.*

A couple of years ago, country artist, Brad Paisley, wrote a song entitled "If I Could Write a Letter to Me." The lyrics depict an older man looking back on his life at the age of seventeen, wishing he could write himself a letter and send it back in time. It's a very fascinating concept. Have you ever thought about that? What would I say to myself at seventeen if I'm forty? Here's the problem: it would probably sound a lot like the stuff your father has already told you.

I have some ideas about what I would say to myself. Maybe things like, "Buy Apple stock! Lot's of it! Sell it in 1991 and buy it back in 2001. You will look like a genius!" What would you say about money if you could go back and talk to yourself? What would you say about investments? What would you say about relationships? You might say, "Watch out for her!" or "That guy is crazy!" Would you say, "Look, I have a few things I need to tell you about life, love, relationships, faith, money and wisdom"?

Obviously, no one can do that. Yet God, in his brilliance, had a higher plan when he designed parents, knowing that one generation would walk the path before another, gaining and imparting wisdom along the way. Take a look at what Solomon says in chapter 4:

> *Listen, my sons, to a father's instruction; pay attention and gain understanding. I give you sound learning, so do not forsake my teaching. When I was a boy in my father's house, still tender, and an only child of my mother, he taught me and said, "Lay hold of my words with all your heart; keep my commands and you will live."*
>
> *(Proverbs 4:1-4)*

Some people say that experience is the best teacher. I don't know if that's completely true. I'll tell you why. Experience is a hard teacher. Experience is a good teacher, I don't doubt that, but it is an expensive teacher. Experience costs you your most valuable commodity— time. Even if you learn from your experiences you don't get a do-over. Experience can teach you a few lessons, but it can cost you twenty years. For some adults it has cost a marriage. For others, it has cost influencing their kids in the right way. For some it has cost a small fortune (or even a big one) and I promise you they find themselves thinking, "If only at eighteen, someone had taught me..." But you can't go back.

That is why Solomon wrote this to young people. We must listen to those who have gone before us. Now, I know what some of you are thinking. "My father is psychotic. He didn't know anything," or "my mother is an alcoholic." Maybe you're thinking, "I had no chance, I didn't even have a father," or "my parents are dysfunctional, they can't even get out of their own way. How am I supposed to learn from them?" Perhaps your parents don't have godly wisdom. Here's what I would say to you. Number one, your parent's don't have to be godly to teach you something. Your parents don't even have to walk with God to teach you something. Now if they are, all the better, but you need to know that you can learn something from those who have gone before you no matter their past or present spiritual state. They still have observations about life, and it may not all be right, but if you listen closely they may teach you some things that make sense.

Do you remember all the times that your father would repeat the same story to you? He would say something like, "I remember the time that I was...", and you would reply with a combination of annoyance and apathy, "Yeah, I've heard this one, Dad, like thirty-eight times." Do you know why he was repeating the story? It wasn't always because he was forgetful. He was trying to communicate something to you that held great importance to him. He told that story over and over because there was value buried somewhere in it that he wanted you to see.

Bad examples are effective teaching tools, as well. Even dysfunctional parents often see the mistakes of their own personal pasts clearly. Whether they are making good choices now or not, you can still learn something from them. Maybe they missed an important lesson early in life and have the scars to prove it. They're worth listening to. Some of you watched your parents make unhealthy choices and find yourself saying, "I saw what happened there. I will never do that. I saw what happens when you go down that road. That's a road I will never travel." The point I would make here is, even if your parents don't seem wise, there are still many lessons to learn from the previous generations. No matter how wise you may think they are, or how foolish they may appear, you are making a huge mistake if you choose to not listen to those who have gone before you. The very same forks in the road that you face were the ones they faced. The wise person learns from the past.

Solomon also knew that when you stand at a fork in the road, there are going to be many voices pulling you in different directions. One of the reasons that it is so easy to make the wrong decision is that not everyone is encouraging you to go the right way. In fact, at many times in your life the majority of voices will be pulling you in the wrong direction. Solomon wrote in Proverbs 1:10:

My son, if sinners entice you, do not give in to them.

Remember the three guys I mentioned earlier: the coach, the athlete and the baseball manager? I could have also talked about preachers, politicians and business leaders. These guys were just famous. That's the only difference. We're all capable of doing the same dumb stuff, and many of us do. As you read that story, you may have found yourself thinking, "How stupid! What a bunch of idiots! How can you blow through $80 million and you're only 39?" Can I tell you something? They're not stupid. It wasn't an IQ issue. They may have had good intentions but they just chose the wrong path. Do you know why? Because there is always going to be somebody on the other side making the wrong path look very appealing. That's what Solomon is saying in verse 10. ***My son, if sinners entice you, do not give in to them.*** You are going to find yourself there. The wrong path is going to look very good. Here's the problem: Happy now doesn't mean happy later.

We all want to be happy but we don't always want to go on a treasure hunt for wisdom. Happy today doesn't mean happy tomorrow. That's the problem. Take the coach, for example. He's fifty-two, riding through the woods with a twenty-five year old woman on the back of his motorcycle, testosterone flowing. What he thought would bring him happiness only led to regret. Why? Because happiness now doesn't always translate into happiness later. We hear the phrase "No money down and no interest for two years," yet we can't afford the product being offered. Once again, we experience regret. Why? Because happiness now doesn't always translate into happiness later. It's true in money, it's true in morals and it's true in relationships. The key is to be wise now, so you can be happy tomorrow. You have to resist buying the lies. You'll hear them everyday. You'll hear them everywhere. You'll hear them on commercials, you'll see them on billboards, and you'll get them from people in your own life.

> *They rejected my advice and paid no attention when I corrected them. Therefore, they must eat the bitter fruit of living their own way, choking on their own schemes. For simpletons turn away from me—to death. Fools are destroyed by their own complacency.*
> *(Proverbs 1:30-32)*

Do you know what complacency is? Complacency is not caring. Anytime advice is given to the young, some will listen and desire wisdom, but there are others who will say, "I don't care." That is why Solomon wrote that they are destroyed by their own complacency. If only they had listened, they would have lived in peace, untroubled by the fear of harm. Proverbs 2:12-13 attaches another huge benefit to wisdom.

> *Wisdom will save you from evil people, from those whose words are twisted.*

There will always be people who twist their words to make things look good that aren't good.

> *These men turn from the right way to walk down dark paths.*
> *(Proverbs 12:13)*

There is the idea of the "paths" again. Solomon urges us to learn from the ideas of others and follow the steps of good men. Stay on the path of the righteous. The truth is, a man can live his life any way he wants, but he can only live it once.

Robert Frost wrote this famous line of poetry:

Two roads diverged in a yellow wood...Yet knowing how way leads on to way, I doubted if I should ever come back.

Do you know what he was saying? "I know that the decision that I make today will turn into the direction I take tomorrow, and that will become the destiny I create for my life." Beware the fork in the road, for the choices you make matter. Choose wisdom. Get all the wisdom you can from God, from previous generations, and from the examples of others. That is what this book is all about. Get all the advice you can. Gain as much wisdom as you can because you have some huge choices ahead and the decisions you make will become the direction you take and the destiny you create. Listen closely and choose well.

Letter Two

Character: The Inside Matters Most

Dear Son,

We live in a world of misplaced priorities. We value the "outside" stuff. We're obsessed with what we can see, measure, wear, touch and compare. We're infatuated with beauty, intoxicated with money and motivated by envy. Your success in life, real success, will come with making sure you value the things that really matter most. Those things can't be held, or measured with a number and they are often unseen. It's the stuff inside that matters most, your character and your integrity.

Over the long haul, your character is who you really are. Most things you possess can be taken away from you, but your integrity can only be given away. Once you give it away it is nearly impossible to ever get it back. Determine early on to be a person of real integrity and what happens on the outside won't really matter.

Character is telling the truth, even when it is easier to tell a lie and it often will be. The person who lies and cheats is only deceiving and robbing himself. The truth can hurt in the short run, but it always pays off in the end. A lie can bring short-term relief, but it will always eventually hurt far more. Plenty of men have been brought down, not by their mistakes, but by compounding their errors with deception and dishonesty.

Character is treating other people with respect and compassion. Treat women with respect. Treat older women as mothers and treat younger women as sisters. Respect them, be kind to them, and be ready to serve and help them. Men, who treat women as objects to be used or people to be manipulated, lack character. Care about those who are weaker or poorer than you. There will always be people who didn't have all the advantages and opportunities that you have had. There will always be people who possess fewer gifts. Don't be prideful. What do you have that you were not given? Don't misuse people. Treat others as if they belong to God Himself, for they do and He is watching.

Character means standing up for what is right. Real men have a sense of what is right and, when needed, they are ready to stand for, fight or defend a noble cause. When injustice is perpetrated, do not feign ignorance or plead that it is not your cause. True, you cannot fight every battle, nor should you, and yes it's true that there will always be cruelty and injustice in the world, but when you can you must stand for what is right and defend those who are being taken advantage of.

Character cannot be bought or sold. It comes from within and it comes from above. Anyone can do the right thing once in a while, but character does the right thing even when it is the hard thing, especially when it is the hard thing. That is what separates people of character from those who lack it.

Your life is ahead of you and yet all too soon it will be behind you. Sooner than you think you will look back on the roads traveled. You will see the relationships and choices that marked your life. You will be remembered by those who knew and loved you. Determine at the beginning of this journey to be remembered for being a man of integrity, a man of character. Tell the truth. Treat others with respect and love, especially the weak. Stand for what is right. It will be easy to lose the way. Most people you meet will be enamored by the "outside" stuff. Never forget, the inside matters most.

Love,

Dad

Chapter Two

Character: The Inside Matters Most

The path of the righteous is like the first gleam of dawn, shining ever brighter till the full light of day. But the way of the wicked is like deep darkness; they do not know what makes them stumble. My son, pay attention to what I say; listen closely to my words. Do not let them out of your sight, keep them within your heart; for they are life to those who find them and health to a man's whole body. Above all else, guard your heart, for it is the wellspring of life.
(Proverbs 4: 18-23)

The next key to gaining wisdom and choosing well is to understand the importance of character and integrity. Solomon draws our attention to another fundamental lesson in Proverbs 4:18-23.

The New Living Translation translates verse 23: *Guard your heart above all else for it determines the course of your life.* A guard is someone who has an important job to do, a cause or person to defend. Solomon wanted the reader to know that his heart is going to be under attack. He must stand guard, watch out and vigilantly protect his heart. This is a serious command to pass along to the next generation.

Solomon uses the word "heart" in the same metaphysical sense that we use it. We often make statements such as, "I love you with all my heart," or "that person put their heart into it." What we're really referring to is our will or consciousness.

Our heart encompasses our emotions, our decisions and our very lives. It is the part of us that makes choices and judgments. Solomon is saying, "You're going to have to guard, watch carefully and protect the contents on the inside." He is declaring that the consistency of your heart is your substance which will determine the course of your life. If you want to know where you're heading then take a good look at your heart because whatever is in your heart will capture the attention of your eyes and determine the direction of your feet. Your heart will determine the course of your life. It is what is on the inside that matters most.

Years ago I heard James Dobson tell a story. Dr. Dobson has been a prominent voice among evangelicals since the 1970's. He has written best-selling books, sold thousands of videos, and established one of the largest Para-church organizations in America. He has counseled Presidents and been courted by politicians. His name is one known by hundreds and thousands of Christians and non-Christians alike all over the world. He told a story about a particular day many years after he had become a well-known psychologist when he received a box. It was kind of an unusual box: inside was a strangely familiar object and a letter. The letter was from a man who was a construction worker in Dobson's hometown. This man worked for a company hired to clear out a dilapidated high school before it was torn down. One of the things removed was an aged trophy case. Dusty trophies from victories won in years past donned its shelves. Great accomplishments memorialized in both plaques and statues sat on glass ledges. Each one with an expectation of being admired for years to come sat unnoticed years later. As this man emptied the trophies from the case there was no one there to claim them. One by one he transferred them to a large garbage can. That day, in a vacant hallway, stood no soul who remembered. No one showed up to recount the hard fought victory epitomized by a medal or the emotional championship win symbolized in a brass cup or the proud moment remembered only by that special trophy in the back. No one was there to claim them. As the man cleared out cases and closets alike, he looked at each trophy before transferring it to the garbage. Then he came across one with James Dobson's name on it.

Jim Dobson had been a senior at that high school when he won some kind of district tennis title. He was awarded a trophy and recognized as a champion tennis player. After it was presented to him it was placed in a trophy case. A few years later it was stuck in a closet where it would sit for decades before meeting the fate of the dumpster. But just by happenstance this guy knew of James Dobson and had read some of his books. After a few moments of thought the man decided to box up the trophy, write a short note, and put them in the mail. A few days later Dobson held a trophy he hadn't looked at in decades. He probably remembered the day that he won it. Maybe, for the first time in years, he thought back to that moment of triumph. It must have been a significant moment to win a championship. He had surely been proud to have his name engraved on the trophy, boldly displayed behind glass for the entire school to see. But when he opened the box, seeing the old trophy again made him realize that it represented a great picture of life. Just like that trophy, most of the awards and accolades we value so much today will be tossed in the garbage tomorrow. It's not that they aren't important or significant or worth celebrating. It's just that they're going to be forgotten in a few years. In that moment, he was reminded that the stuff on the inside is what matters most of all.

I have a good friend named Greg Thiel. For several years he was the athletic director and track coach at our high school in Clearwater. Coach Thiel has been around. In fact, he used to coach track on the collegiate level at the University of South Florida. He led their track teams to multiple conference titles and even won Coach of the Year honors. A few years later, following a radical and life-changing encounter with God, he came to serve at our high school. After a short time our track teams were performing very well under Coach Thiel's direction. Our girls won the regional championship and finished as one of the top teams in the state. They were recognized with a large trophy which we proudly placed at the entrance of our school in a case. About a week later when I was talking with Coach Thiel and congratulating him on the notable victory, he mentioned something I thought was pretty insightful. He said, "Pastor, as I was sitting in the middle of that meet adding up the scores, it became clear to me that we were going to win this thing." He continued, "So there I was, laser focused on every score that came in, when one of our runners walked up to me and asked me a question about how she could be certain of God's will in a particular situation in her life. My first thought was 'Seriously, we're about to win a big championship here, can you wait?' But Pastor, I knew better. So I took a few minutes to talk with her about how she could gain the wisdom and clarity that God wanted to give her, and then quickly jumped back into the mindset of the meet. Later that night, as I was recounting the events of the day, it dawned on me. The most important win, on or off the track, was in the life of that one athlete whose deep desire to conform to the will of God in her life sent her looking for wisdom." He said to me, "Years from now when all of the trophies are forgotten, the fact that one student was spurred to seek lasting truth in the middle of a momentary victory will be the greatest victory of all." I thought, "Man, you're right." It's the stuff inside that lasts. It's the stuff inside that matters most.

So what can we learn about character? Why is it so important to guard our hearts? Here are several key questions about character that Solomon answers:

What is Character?

To do what is right and just is more acceptable to the Lord than sacrifice.
(Proverbs 21:3)

Character is doing what is right. Solomon is saying that doing the right thing is more important to God than taking part in any religious observance. In other words it is more important that we DO what is right and DO what is just than just showing up at church. Sacrificing was a good thing in Solomon's day, with a good purpose, and attending church is a wonderful thing for God's people to do. But these are still outside decisions that should be made because of what lies on the inside. When a person does the right thing often and consistently enough, you look at their life and say, "That person has character."

Before this sounds too easy, let me add one more phrase to our definition of character. Character is doing the right thing *even when it's the hard thing*. Did you catch that? Go back and reread the last part of that definition. That is the real difference in a person who has character. They do the right thing even when it is the hard thing. When you think about it, everybody does the right thing some of the time. Serial killers do the right thing occasionally. Liars don't always lie. Thieves don't steal every day. Adulterers can go some time without committing adultery.

Everybody does the right thing once in a while. The question is, do you do the right thing when it's the hard thing? Do you do the right thing when it's not easy? It's pretty simple to do the right thing when everyone is watching, when the payoff is clear or when the wrong thing would hurt. But when you are faced with a hard decision, a costly decision, do you still do the right thing? Character is doing the right thing even when it's the hardest thing you've ever done.

This brings us to precisely why you've got to guard your heart. In this sinful world it can be easy to find yourself deceived. Sometimes you're going to be tricked and other times you might be fooled into taking a short cut. Character is refusing that shortcut. Character is doing the right thing even when it is the hard thing.

Chuck Colson passed away in the spring of 2012. He had lived a life of Christian activism and was a prolific author and profound thinker. But most people know that before Colson was a renowned Christian leader, he was best known for his role in the Watergate scandal in the early 1970's. As Nixon's infamous "hatchet man," he had his hand in backroom political maneuvers that targeted opponents and secured political power for Colson and his friends, most notably the President. He was the go-to guy for the 'Dirty Trick Squad', the kind that specialized in planting false information, spreading rumors, and destroying reputations. When the scandal began to unfold, Colson was caught in the web. He would be indicted and forced to leave the White House in disgrace. During this time he became a Christian and, before his case actually went to trial, his conversion and newfound faith became public knowledge and the source of widespread public discussion. Many scoffed. Most Americans cynically dismissed Colson's conversion as a publicity stunt, another "foxhole conversion" from someone trying to avoid the consequences of their actions. But if ever there was an authentic change of heart, this was it. Colson would spend the rest of his life devoted to Christian ministry, especially to the imprisoned, and advancing the cause of Christ. But first, Colson would face a major test of character, one that would reveal he was genuine, and that, no doubt, opened the door for a lifetime of impact.

Prior to his trial, Colson was invited to address numerous gatherings where he spoke of his newfound faith. During this same time, he and his lawyers were battling the charges that had now been levied against him by the federal government. The atmosphere was deeply divisive and Colson was one of the few that had actually been caught and could be tried. The public and the government alike were out of for blood. Many of the charges against Colson were false. Most of them being the result of an aggressive prosecution intent on making someone pay for the political misdeeds of the Nixon White House. Colson and his legal team felt confident that they would win in the end, and that Colson could then move on with his new life. The trial was about four weeks away.

It was during this time that Colson was invited to speak at a prayer breakfast where he openly shared his testimony about coming to faith in Christ. Near the end of his remarks he felt compelled to address the very public legal battle in which he was engaged. He wanted to assure his audience that he was, in fact, innocent. So at the end of his speech he intended to express the sentiment that he knew in his heart that he was not guilty of the crimes for which he had been indicted. This statement would have been true. Instead, he inadvertently inserted the word "most." His statement came out, "In my heart I know that I am not guilty of *most* of the crimes that I have been indicted for." His heart sank. He had misspoken. He didn't mean to use the word "most" but he had. He quickly stammered and corrected his misstatement, hopeful that no one had caught the misstep. After all, it was a friendly crowd and no one, not even the press, said a thing afterwards. But Colson could not shake the feeling that what he had mistakenly said was really closer to the truth than what he had planned to say. No, he wasn't guilty of the crimes that he had been indicted for, but he was guilty of other awful things.

After a weekend of wrestling within himself, he called his lawyer and informed him that he now intended to plead guilty for another crime, one he wasn't even charged for. His lawyers thought he was crazy. They tried to talk him out of it, but Colson knew the truth: he had released secretive information in order to discredit a political opponent. He would plead guilty to this charge, one he brought against himself, and as a result became the first person to be convicted in the Watergate scandal and one of the few that actually went to prison. Colson knew that he might have beaten the original charges had he just kept silent, but that he would never really be free.[2] After spending almost three years in prison, Colson emerged from that ordeal a better and stronger man. His prison time would introduce him to a new life's purpose. Once released, he spent a lifetime ministering to the incarcerated and their families. Perhaps no person ever did more to bring hope to imprisoned souls around the world than Chuck Colson. God gave him a larger platform than ever to speak the truth. For the next forty years he became an intellectual and ethical giant in the Christian world. Chuck Colson has left a legacy that will last all because he chose to do the right thing even though it was the hard thing. Now that is character.

What Does Character Do?

Now that we have locked down the fact that character does the right thing, what exactly does that mean? What is the right thing? If you read through the Proverbs on character, three things keep simmering to the top.

Character tells the truth.

The people in Solomon's day were as adept at concealing, disguising and equivocating as we are today. That is why Solomon wrote about the importance of truth and integrity. Character tells the truth even and especially when it is hard.

Perhaps you have heard this famous story about George Washington, the father of our country. It first appeared in an elementary school textbook in 1806 and while historians debate the historical accuracy, the story became famous as a moral tale that emphasized the virtue of honesty. George was just a boy when his father was given an expensive cherry tree shipped all the way from Europe. He planted that cherry tree in his large orchard and was especially proud of it. Deciding to put his son in charge, he instructed George to take special care of his cherished tree. One day, as luck would have it, George was also given a hatchet. As boys will do, George put the hatchet to good use. He cut and chopped one thing after another for no other reason than his young mind told him that some things just needed to be cut. That's the way a boy thinks, right? So he started cutting and eventually, you guessed it, he cut down his father's prized cherry tree. After it fell to the ground, George went and hid.

A short time later his dad found him. He asked his son, "George, who cut down the cherry tree?" Young George took a moment and realized that he had two choices. He could conceal the truth and probably postpone judgment for a short time, or he could tell the truth. Young George swallowed hard and he said, "Father, I cannot tell a lie. I cut down the cherry tree." George's father took his son by the shoulders and looked him in the eyes and said something like, "Son, I want you to know that I'm proud of you for telling the truth. I would rather have a son who tells the truth when it's hard than to have a thousand cherry trees."[3] Telling the truth always matters. As you know, George eventually became a decorated Revolutionary War general and the first President of the United States. Young George learned a hard lesson on honesty in his father's orchard and the character it built went on to take him far.

Lying is spoken about many times in the Book of Proverbs. We all know what it's like to tell an outrageous lie and what it's like to deal in shades of truth and deception. Look at Proverbs 11:1.

> *The Lord abhors dishonest scales, but accurate weights are his delight.*
> *(Proverbs 11:1)*

Before the development of modern currency people conducted their enterprises through trade and bartering, often using scales and weights. For instance, I might bring something of value to you and you might give something of value to me in exchange. You might bring a certain weight of silver to me and in return I would give you a specific weight of wheat. These people used weights and scales every day to do business. In those days dishonest people made loopholes to deceive and fool others by using faulty weights. They would take the weights, hollow them out and replace them with a false bottom. This way people could be tricked out of getting the price they deserved for their trade. This was a common cheating method in those days.

Thus lying and cheating are not new. Cheating on taxes is not a new idea and adding "fine print" is not a new practice; it just looks different in different cultures. People have always looked for an edge. They've always looked to get ahead in some way. Solomon tells us that God cares about the weights. God hates a dishonest scale, but accurate weights are His delight. You know what that means? Tell the truth. Just because you can get away with it doesn't make it right. Just because you can bury it in the fine print and fool somebody that's gullible, doesn't mean that it pleases God. God knows the truth when He hears it. People of good character are people who speak the truth even when it costs them something. Listen to all these verses about scales and balances.

Honest scales and balances are from the Lord; all the weights in the bag are of his making.
(Proverbs 16:11)

Differing weights and differing measures— the Lord detests them both.
(Proverbs 20:10)

Food gained by fraud tastes sweet to a man, but he ends up with a mouth full of gravel.
(Proverbs 20:17)

In other words, something can taste good today but it will taste bad tomorrow. You can lie today and get away with something, but in the end it will catch up to you.

The Lord detests differing weights, and dishonest scales do not please him.
(Proverbs 20:23)

God is watching! And character tells the truth!

A scoundrel and villain, who goes about with a corrupt mouth, who winks with his eye, signals with his feet and motions with his fingers,
(Proverbs 6:12-13)

This verse isn't about a third base coach motioning to a player in baseball or a fidgety toddler. It's about someone who is in a business deal winking their eye, crossing their fingers, or tapping their partner on the foot. They are signaling to someone in order to deceive someone else. Maybe someone is trying to sell a house and saying, "No, the roof doesn't leak, does it, honey?" And they wink with the eye or signal with the finger. They are hiding the truth. Proverbs calls that a corrupt mouth. Character is telling the truth no matter what. Everyone tells the truth some of the time, but what separates a person of character from the rest is that they tell the truth all of the time. They tell the truth even when it's hard. You can tell a lie and have short-term gain, but God promises that if you tell the truth, you will have long-term gain. It may hurt you today, but if you tell the truth, you are a person of character.

Character stands for justice.

Character will work for what is right.

> *The righteous care about justice for the poor, but the wicked have no such concern.*
> *(Proverbs 29:7)*

Solomon mentions the poor here because they are the persons least able to ensure fair treatment for themselves. The Bible says that a righteous person, a person of character, cares about what is right.

Now there are many people today who go around talking about how they work for justice, but what they really mean is that they'll find a loophole to get you what you want. That's not justice. Just because something is legal doesn't make it right. Just because you can get away with it doesn't make it fair. In fact, the word "just" according to Webster means "acting or being in conformity with what is morally upright or good." Guess who determines that? God does. Something is true or right because it mirrors the character of God. Something is right because it's like God and conforms to His character. Look at these verses:

> *A wicked man accepts a bribe in secret to pervert the course of justice.*
> *(Proverbs 17:23)*

> *It is not good to be partial to the wicked or to deprive the innocent of justice.*
> *(Proverbs 18:5)*

> *It is not good to punish an innocent man, or to flog officials for their integrity.*
> *(Proverbs 17:26)*

> *A corrupt witness mocks at justice, and the mouth of the wicked gulps down evil.*
> *(Proverbs 19:28)*

> *Do not testify against your neighbor without cause, or use your lips to deceive. Do not say, "I'll do to him as he has done to me; I'll pay that man back for what he did."*
> *(Proverbs 4:28-29)*

Have you ever thought to yourself, "Somebody did me wrong, so I'll do them wrong?" The Bible says a person of character does not act on that notion. Just like your momma told you, "Two wrongs don't make a right." If she didn't tell you, I will. It's always right to do the right thing and it's always wrong to do the wrong thing. Character has a strong sense of justice.

Character cares for the weak.

A person of character cares for people who don't have as much money, influence, or intellectual prowess. God says, "The way you treat other people matters."

> *He who oppresses the poor shows contempt for their Maker, but whoever is kind to the needy honors God.*
> ***(Proverbs 14:31)***

Often, people oppress others simply because they can get away with it. The Bible says that if you oppress the poor, you show contempt for the one who made them. You're basically saying that they don't matter, but God has said that they do matter! By thinking in this manner, you are showing contempt for God. *...whoever is kind to the needy honors God.* Look at these verses:

> *If a man shuts his ears to the cry of the poor, he too will cry out and not be answered.*
> *(Proverbs 21:13)*

> *Do not exploit the poor because they are poor and do not crush the needy in court, for the Lord will take up their case and will plunder those who plunder them.*
> *(Proverbs 22:22-23)*

> *Do not move an ancient boundary stone or encroach on the fields of the fatherless,*
> *(Proverbs 23:10)*

In ancient times people marked their territory with a boundary stone. Those who lacked moral character would often be found moving the boundary stones of those who didn't have the means to fight them. They would steadily increase their own territory by inching in on someone else's. No one surveyed the land back then. Property ownership wasn't marked on a map and held in a government office. Dishonest people often got away with this. But God says, no way!

> *... for their Defender is strong; he will take up their case against you.*
> *(Proverbs 23:11)*

You don't want to have God sitting on the opposite side of the courtroom from you, trust me. God commands us to care for those who have less than we do, or may not be as clever as we are, or lack the resources available to us. We must treat them just as God wants them to be treated. That's character. It tells the truth, it stands for what is right and it cares about people who have less power and influence.

Why Does Character Matter?

"Guard your heart..." Why did Solomon say this? Because Solomon knew that failing to guard your heart will lead you down one path of compromise after another. We have all been tempted to take the wrong path. There will always be choices that you know are right but you're hesitant to make because the outcome might be painful, the consequences tough or the result unpleasant. You see, telling the truth when it hurts *is* the hard thing. Standing for what is right *is* going to end up costing you at some point in your life. It might even hurt someone you love. But reaching down deep inside your heart, where the root of your character is buried in the soil of your soul, in order to muster the courage to make the right choice even when it hurts...well, that's character. God says, "Guard your heart. Make sure you care about what is right. Make sure you care for the weak. Make sure you tell the truth." Why? Because your character will help set the compass for the direction your life will take.

You're not just making a choice: you're determining a course. You're not only making a decision: you're choosing a destination. Sometimes we know what the right thing is, it's just plain hard to do it. If you break off that relationship, it will hurt. It may hurt you emotionally or it may disappoint someone else, but you already know it is the right thing to do. So why haven't you done it? Most likely it's because you know that it's going to be hard.

Most people don't want to do the hard thing. They just want to be happy. They want to do the easy thing. The bottom line is: the choices you make determine the course of your life. My character determines my course. Your character determines yours.

We saw Proverbs 4:18 at the beginning of this chapter. Look closely at it one more time.

> *The path of the righteous is like the first gleam of dawn, shining ever brighter till the full light of day.*
> *(Proverbs 4:18)*

Have you ever been up at dawn when the first gleam of light is faint? It's still pretty dark outside. You can't see much. But as that first ray leaks over the horizon, you know that pretty soon the sun will be in the sky and you'll see it all.

That's what the path of the righteous is like. As you start down that path you can't see how it's all going to end. Things are still pretty dark and still pretty foggy. There's just a little light on the horizon. But if you choose to do what is right, God promises that eventually you're going to be walking in the full light of day.

It's the very path you're choosing that will determine the very outcome you will experience. If you choose to do what is right, just as the sun gets brighter and brighter and brighter, your path will get brighter and brighter, and clearer and clearer. If you are a young person reading this book, you have some advantages on me. You can probably run faster than I can and have a whole lot more hair. But can I tell you one of the big advantages that I have? It is the same advantage that Solomon had. When you live enough years you can look back and see where certain paths have led. I can look back and see how certain choices, the right choices, took me on paths that led me to blessed places. Just like the gleam of light at dawn, it got brighter and brighter. But it started with a small simple choice to do the right thing. I can also see where some choices led me down dark alleys where I didn't want to go.

So here's a fact; you're not just making a decision. You're choosing a destination. You will face some huge choices. You may be facing one now. Usually, it isn't the rightness or wrongness of a choice that makes it most difficult, it's the hardness of it. Character is doing the right thing even when it's the hard thing. If you do, God will lead you to the brightness of day. Colson had to spend a couple of years in jail, but he did the right thing. And you know what happened? During the next 40 years of his life God gave him tremendous influence around the world. It just might be that if he had compromised then for short-term gain he never would have had the long-term blessing of God on his life.

Do the right thing and God will lead you to the brightness of His approval and His blessing. That's a promise. That's a destination that's worth pursuing.

Letter Three

Communication: Watch Your Words

Dear Son,

Sometimes the line between success or failure, blessing or cursing, even life or death, can be very thin. And in life it is often the words we say that make the difference. There is that much power in your tongue. The Bible says the tongue holds the power of life or death. It really does.

That does not mean that our words hold creative power like God. We cannot in one sense create something out of nothing simply by our words. And yet, our words do hold great power and there is a real sense in which our words create worlds. Encourage someone and watch his or her world change. Criticize someone and his or her entire day can be shattered. Words matter, more than you can imagine. You can build up or tear down and that power lies in the words you use.

The book of James compares the tongue to the rudder of a ship, small but powerful. The rudder is slight but its turn can steer a ship toward the rocks or open water, toward icy cliffs or balmy seas. Just turn the rudder and everything changes. And so it is with your words. Words change everything. Spoken. Texted. Emailed. Posted. Words create worlds.

The right word at the right time to the right person for the right reason can usher you into success, favor, even love. The wrong word spoken to the wrong person at the wrong time for the wrong reason (or any such combination) can sever a relationship forever, destroy trust and create a chasm that can take years to overcome. Words are just that powerful so use them wisely. Your words can open more doors than any key. Your words can create more havoc than any explosive. Watch your mouth, it will steer your life like a ship's rudder.

Beware of words spoken in anger. Few things can make a person look like a fool quicker than foolish words spoken in anger. Since words matter so much use them carefully. You will have to eat them from time to time so make them as sweet as possible. Think before you speak. A line you think is funny can devastate another person. Flippant words spoken in jest can do real harm. They can mar your testimony. Weeks, even years of faithful toil can be undone by a careless word. The careers of gifted men and women have been ruined by a careless word. Great intellectuals, skilled politicians, renowned talents have all been undone, banished to obscurity and disgrace because in a single moment, in the twinkling of an eye, a careless word brought them down. You have the right to remain silent. I recommend you use that right often.

Make sure your words are truthful. God hates lying lips. Beware the gossip. There will always be people with stories to tell. They are careless, indifferent and even cruel as they hurl their words into the air, trashing other's reputations. Watch out for such people and avoid them. Run in the other direction. Treat the reputations of others as if it were your own. Do not say things are true when you don't know if they are. Even true things do not always need to be repeated. It has been said that people cannot be judged by what others say about them, but they can be judged by what they say about others.

Use your words to build up other people. The right word can diffuse anger. The right word can brighten someone's day or even save a life. Our mouths can serve no greater cause than to spread the good news about Christ. Such words can not only save a life, but also alter eternity. So you see there really is the power of life and death in your tongue. Learn to say no. Learn to say yes. Learn sometimes to say nothing at all. It can be the difference between life and death.

Love,

Dad

Chapter Three
Communication:
Watch Your Words

He who guards his lips guards his life, but he who speaks rashly will come to ruin.
(Proverbs 13:3)

People can do powerful things. It's amazing what some people have tamed, what challenges they have met and the discipline some athletes display. But there is one challenge that is too much for all of us. It pins us to the mat. It laughs at our discipline. It ridicules our attempts to tame it. According to the Bible, it is the most difficult thing for a man to bridle. It is more difficult to control than sexual urges or physical appetites. It is your mouth. It is controlling the power of the tongue.

The Book of James says that while men can tame wild animals such as lions and tigers, the most difficult thing to tame is one of the smallest organs in your body. It is the tongue and like a rudder to a ship it will steer your life.

The truth is, we all struggle to control the tongue in our mouths. You've said stupid things and so have I. We've all engaged in hurtful discourse, reckless comments and fictitious talk. So it's no surprise that amidst all of the advice that Solomon was passing on to the next generation, he would have some counsel to give about your speech. Watch your words and your communication.

In Proverbs 13:3 Solomon wrote:

> *He who guards his lips guards his life, but he who speaks rashly will come to ruin.*

Those who guard their lips are guarding their very life, and those who speak rashly are guaranteed ruin. The New Living Translation says it like this:

> *Open your mouth and it ruins everything...*

Certainly many people have proven that to be true. Solomon is warning us to *guard* our mouths. When someone posts a guard it means there is a perceived threat. Where there is a guard, something is at risk and needs protection. Usually a guard is protecting against a threat on the outside, but when it comes to guarding our lips, it's because there is something on the inside that could come out and do great damage. This guard is looking on the inside and saying, "Watch your words." The Bible says that the man who guards his lips is literally guarding his life. Solomon sums it up in Proverbs 18:21 saying,

> *The tongue has the power of life and death...*

It doesn't get bigger than that! Your mouth, your tongue, your words have the power to bring life or death. Have you heard the phrase: *Words create worlds*? God's Word spoke the world into being. Now we're not God, and just because we say something doesn't mean it will come true, but our words still hold power. You see, the right word at the right time creates a certain world. The wrong word at the wrong time creates a different world. Your words hold the power of life and death.

How Do We Speak Words of Life?

If your words are that important, if they are powerful enough to create life, then you need to learn how to speak those life-giving words. Solomon knew the difference between words that bring life and those that bring death. He used the words 'mouth', 'lips', 'words' and 'tongue' a combined one hundred fifty times in the Book of Proverbs. That's almost five times in each chapter. If you gather all of that insight and counsel, it can be collectively summarized it into three main points of advice on how to guard your lips and create life with your words.

Speak Carefully

If you want to guard your lips and preserve your words for only those that give life then you must speak carefully. What does that mean? Well, the opposite of careful is careless. Proverbs 13:3 says, *...he who speaks rashly...* What the Hebrew text is literally saying there is 'he who opens his mouth wide'. We've all heard it said that someone has a big mouth. Maybe you've said it or it's been said about you. Proverbs 13:3 tells us that if we open your mouths too wide it will bring ruin. Of course it's not the physiological size of your mouth that is referred to here, but the carelessness of your words. So right off the bat, Proverbs warns us to be careful, to think before we speak and to choose our words wisely.

Perhaps one of the biggest lies taught to children is: "Sticks and stones may break my bones but words can never hurt me." You and I both know that long after the bruises caused by sticks and stones heal, the lesions left by vicious words produce great pain. You can probably still recall words that were spoken to you years ago, words that still create incredible pain. Be careful what you say. Words matter.

Have you ever been in a situation where someone is speaking and you think to yourself, "Good grief. Do they not have a filter? Is there some kind of disconnect between their head and their mouth?" Your Heavenly Father is saying to you, "Filter what you say. Be careful. Think about your words for they hold incredible power."

I want to give you just a couple of tools to help you be more careful in your speech. They all come directly out of Proverbs and may seem rudimentary and very practical, but they are powerful when put to use. The first one is: *Speak less*. Use fewer words. Don't run your mouth to fill up quiet space. The more you speak, the more inevitable it is that you will say something stupid. Those who talk a lot usually end up regretting something they've said. Proverbs contains many verses concerning the amount of our speech.

> *A truly wise person uses few words; a person with understanding is even tempered.*
> (Proverbs **17:27**)

He doesn't lose control and speak without thinking.

> *Even fools are thought to be wise when they keep silent; with their mouths shut they seem intelligent.*
> ***(Proverbs 17:28)***

By just using fewer words, your IQ goes up. Speak more and your IQ goes down, at least the perception of it does. People often see a quiet person and think, "Well there's a bright guy. He must be thoughtful and very introspective." You might be as dumb as a rock but because you use fewer words than the next guy you're going to seem smarter than you really are. Don't get me wrong here. Communication is one of God's greatest gifts. I am communicating right now. There is a time and a place to speak, but so often and in so many cases we simply speak too much.

Did you know that there is no law in any state or country that requires you to say everything that you're thinking? It's true. No law exists that requires you to articulate every thought or opinion you have. You don't have to show up to every argument you are invited to. You have the right to remain silent. Use it. You will look a lot smarter.

Calvin Coolidge was President of the United States in the early part of the twentieth century and was famous for saying: *"I was never hurt by anything I didn't say."*[4] Most of us have never been hurt by something we didn't say but how many of us wish we could take back words that we have already spoken? How many times have you thought back on something you've said and cringed? You've probably said to yourself, "What in the world was I thinking?" The truth is, you weren't. We've all been careless with our words.

I mentioned the well-known Christian author Chuck Colson in Chapter Two. When he passed away in the spring of 2012, I went back and reread his biography, *Born Again*. It was the first of many books Colson would write and thirty years had passed since I had first read it. It was published in the late 1970's and detailed his spiritual conversion after the political scandal known as Watergate. One of the most infamous scandals in American history, Watergate brought down the entire Nixon administration and forced the first and only resignation of a President in U.S. history. President Nixon and his administration were embroiled in numerous misdeeds and Colson was a part of the inner circle. Although he had resigned from Nixon's administration at the end of the first term, he still remained one of the President's inside confidants and continued talking with the President on a regular basis. As the scandal evolved, the political acrimony became white hot. Accusations were hurled and indictments were handed down. Colson was one of the first indicted and would plead guilty to the obstruction of justice and go to prison for seven months.

In his book *Born Again*, Colson recounted those days, reflecting on how the scandal had become front-page news and how his own role and integrity were impugned. Everything was coming down. But then something was revealed that surprised even him. He thought that he had been privy to everything that went on inside the White House until a bombshell dropped. He recounts sitting in his office when the news broke: The White House had a secret taping mechanism that had recorded every conversation that took place in the Oval Office for the prior four years. He had no idea that every exchange he had with the President had been secretly recorded. Every word was on record. Every impromptu discussion, every off-colored joke, every analysis of a colleague and every bit of gossip spoken were all taped and would soon be made public.[5]

Can you imagine if everything you said over the last four years was recorded somewhere? How would you feel today if I said to you, "Oh, guess what? Everything you have said over the past couple of years was recorded and we've got a transcript that we're going to release tomorrow for the whole world to read. Everything you said about so and so, every word you spoke 'just between us', every joke, every quip, every observation you made is on tape." That would be awful! Every one of us would be scared to death. We'd be begging for it not to be released.

But in a sense, isn't there already a record? God knows every word we've spoken, and Jesus said that we will be held accountable for all of them. Our words matter to God and He is paying attention. Many people have said things in private that later brought them down in public. What Solomon is saying to us is, "Be careful what you say," and the first step in being careful is to just speak less. You see, it isn't the tapes that brought down President Nixon, it is what was on the tapes that made him fall. It's what you say that will end up doing great damage. Look at these Proverbs:

> *Do you see a man who speaks in haste? There is more hope for a fool than for him.*
> *(Proverbs 29:20)*

> *So avoid a man who talks too much.*
> *(Proverbs 20:19)*

> *Too much talk leads to sin. Be sensible and keep your mouth shut.*
> *(Proverbs 10:19)*

The second key to being careful with your words is: *Listen more than you speak.* In fact, James says this:

> *Be quick to listen, and be slow to speak.*
> *(James 1:19)*

Most of us do exactly the opposite of what James advises. We are quick to speak and slow to listen. By nature, we want to talk first and listen second. But the Bible says that wisdom comes from listening first and then talking. Now here is some advanced research that I know you will find helpful: if you will look in the mirror, you will see that you have two ears and only one mouth. Two ears…one mouth. Two is always greater than one. Every morning when you walk into the bathroom and stare in the mirror, it should be a reminder to be quick to listen and slow to speak.

Several years ago, Stephen Covey wrote a book entitled *The Seven Habits of Highly Effective People.* In that book he analyzed what he saw as the habits of executives and leaders, not only in the business world but also in other professions.

He detailed seven key habits that all leaders must exhibit. One of those habits was: *Seek to understand before being understood.*[6] Most of us want to be understood first. We want to state our opinion and make sure everyone listening understands it. That's why you practice chewing people out when you're in the shower, right? Or maybe driving down the road, you rehearse what you might say if you could give that someone a piece of your mind. We never practice listening, do we? Have you ever thought to yourself, "Boy, what would it be like if I just sat down and listened to them for forty minutes?" No, instead we practice the speech we would love to give them if they would sit quiet for forty minutes and listen to us. Why? It is because we want to be understood. But a principle of success says: understand first, listen first, and then seek to speak clearly. Listen more than you speak. Try to understand what the other person is saying before you open your mouth. This is an important habit in business and in all of life.

Parents love to give lectures, don't they? We can't wait to give a well-crafted lecture. Our kid walks in the kitchen saying something we disagree with and we've got our lecture ready. We've got a whole file of them handed down from the generations. And yet we wonder why we find ourselves saying the same dumb things our parents said to us. We just pull one out and download it. How many times has a kid walked in the house and said, "I hate school!" Cue the lecture. That was all we needed to hear. Then we say something stupid like, "Don't you know how lucky you are to be able to go to school? Did you know I walked to school eight miles each way every day without shoes and in the snow? Yes, it snowed every day! And do you know all of the sacrifices I've made to send you to school? How can you even think about quitting?" Boom! And away we go with the lecture and do you know what? Communication shuts down. If we had only spent time listening first, maybe we would have found out that he failed a test on Monday and someone called him stupid when he got the grade on Wednesday. Now he's struggling with his self-image and feels like he'll never make it. If we had spent time listening we would have known what the problem really was and then we could have said something helpful instead of inserting a lecture.

When we try to speak first and listen second or when we seek to be understood rather than to understand, our words have very little impact and hold very little wisdom. If you want to be careful with your words, as Solomon tells us to do, then listen first. Strive to understand what the other person thinks and what they're trying to say, and then attempt to be understood. Listen and then speak. That goes for emails, texts, Facebook messages and any other media outlet they might invent tomorrow. You see, lecturing is easier when the communication is one-way. That's what all of these are, one-way avenues to speak your mind or drop your opinion. There is no give and take. Even if someone sends you a reply five minutes later, it is still not give and take. Whether you send an email, a Facebook message or a text, you are giving a speech. It might just be that you are transmitting the facts, like "The meeting was changed from 4:00 to 4:30", and that's fine. But when you have to deal with nuanced conversation, when something requires listening first and then speaking, these modes of communication fail.

In some businesses, more time is wasted emailing messages back and forth that could be saved if people would get up from behind their keyboards, walk three feet down the hallway into the next office, and have a conversation. I can say that because I have messed up here many times. When you send information one way, there's no listening, and that's why problems sometimes escalate. If you manage people or if you supervise people, can I give you one word of counsel? Don't use email or one-way communication to correct and reprove people. That's a terrible way to do it. If you have something critical to say you need to look them in the eye. You can speak directly to them and they will have the opportunity to speak directly to you. This way you will better understand what is really going on. You must seek to understand and then you can be understood. This gives you a chance to speak wisely and carefully.

Great salesmen understand this. Successful salesmen don't sell products, they sell solutions to people's problems. The ones who know this make a lot of money. Do you know how to know what people's problems are? You have to listen. You are never going to find them out by talking. The only way to learn more about anything or anyone is by listening to what someone has said or by reading what someone else has written.

Great lawyers can argue the other side's case better than the opposing counsel. They write the other guy's case before they write their own. Why? It's because they will never win a case without listening and knowing the argument of the other side. They look at the data from all angles, and then they can seek to be understood. This is not new wisdom. The Bible says it again and again.

So first of all, you must speak carefully. Listen, and understand the importance of listening. Use fewer words. Don't say as much. If you use fewer words and listen to people, you will inevitably speak more carefully.

Speak Truthfully

Here is a second bit of advice from the Book of Proverbs. If you want your words to be "life-giving," you must not only speak carefully, but you must speak truthfully. You would suspect the Bible has a lot to say about this, and it does.

The Lord detests lying lips, but he delights in men who are truthful.
(Proverbs 12:22)

Truthful lips endure forever, but a lying tongue lasts only a moment.
(Proverbs 12:19)

Dishonesty can bring temporary relief from a situation or a consequence, but the relief will only last for a moment and ultimately it will bring permanent pain. The truth, however, might bring temporary pain but it will bring permanent relief. Truthful lips endure, lying lips last only for a moment. Take a look at these verses:

A truthful witness saves lives, but a false witness is deceitful.
(Proverbs 14:25)

Kings take pleasure in honest lips; they value a man who speaks the truth.

(Proverbs 16:13)

A lying tongue hates those it hurts, and a flattering mouth works ruin.

(Proverbs 26:28)

There are six things the Lord hates, seven that are detestable to him:...a lying tongue.

(Proverbs 6:16)

Out of the seven things that the Lord says he hates in Proverbs 6, two of them concern lips that do not speak truthfully. One of them is a lying tongue and another is a witness that brings false testimony.

Now we all know that lying and dishonesty are problems, but there is something else that we see all the time and don't often think of as lying, but it is. It is a practice mentioned throughout the Book of Proverbs. It is called gossip. Gossiping is when you say something about another person, true or untrue, that is harmful and unkind. Why do we do it? The Book of Proverbs says that it "tastes" good to us. It's kind of like junk food. It's cheap entertainment and makes us feel better about ourselves. Gossip is a dangerous pastime. Look at these verses:

> *A gossip betrays a confidence, but a trustworthy man keeps a secret.*
>
> *(Proverbs 11:13)*

> *A perverse man stirs up dissension, and a gossip separates close friends.*
>
> *(Proverbs 16:28)*

> *The words of a gossip are like choice morsels; (They taste good.) they go down to a man's inmost parts.*
> *(Proverbs 18:8)*

> *Without wood a fire goes out; without gossip a quarrel dies down.*
>
> *(Proverbs 26:20)*

Isn't it true? Gossip separates friendships. People stir up dissension with their words. Solomon advises us to avoid this kind of talk, to abstain from conversation that is harmful and malicious.

I remember a conversation I overheard once where two ladies were discussing a certain situation. One lady said, "Tell me a bit more," and the other lady replied, "Well, I've already told you more than I know." There are a whole lot of people who have told more than they knew. Sometimes we justify our gossip by saying that the information is true. But just because it is true doesn't mean that it needs to be talked about.

We've all heard the saying, "Think before you speak." Someone came up with an acrostic for the word THINK that has taught me to ask five questions before I say anything. If you will take the time to ask yourself these five questions, I think you will be saying a whole lot less.

T – Is It True?

I don't mean that someone else told you that it's true. Do you know for a fact that it's true? By the way, not everything on the Internet is true. Did you know that? Just because someone in church sent you an email that guarantees an immediate blessing if you forward it to one hundred people and then says you'll get leprosy if you don't, doesn't mean it's true. IT'S NOT. It doesn't happen. It's a lie. You can delete it. You must always ask yourself, "Is this true?" Do I know it is true?

H – Is This Helpful?

Does what you are about to say help anyone? Will it help the person you are talking about? Will it help another person?

I – Is It Inspiring?

Is what I am about to say inspiring? Will it make all involved want to do better, live better? Is it an encouragement to somebody?

N – Is It Necessary?

Is there some reason why I need to share it?

K – Is It Kind?

If what I am about to say ended up on a transcript that got released publicly, would I be embarrassed? Is it kind?

If you would stop to think, "Is this true? Is it helpful? Is it inspiring? Is it necessary? Is it kind?" I promise you will be talking a lot less about other people than you would ordinarily do. The Bible says to speak carefully and speak truthfully. And then Solomon offers a third piece of advice about life-giving words.

Speak Constructively

Yours words can either build people up or tear people down. They are either constructive or destructive. Your words have that much power.

> *Worry weighs a person down, but an encouraging word cheers a person up.*
> *(Proverbs 12:25)*

Isn't that amazing? While worry weighs people down, an encouraging word has the power to completely transform a person's mood. It can brighten someone's day. Choose to be positive and seek to build people up.

I heard about a young man who became a renowned photographer. He had built a successful career around his craft. At one point someone asked him the question, "How did you get into photography?" He said, "Well, it goes back to my childhood. Back in the day when you had actual film, someone let me borrow a camera. I went out and took a picture. I went out and took rolls of pictures." He continued, "After we had them developed, my mom spread them all out on a table. They were terrible, absolutely horrible. There were thumbs in the middle and most every subject had their head chopped off." He went on to say, "There were probably only ten that were even slightly good. But there was this one. My mother took that one picture and said, 'Wow! Look at this picture! You got the lighting just right! Look at how you framed that expression! Look at all you captured in that picture!' She went on and on for a couple of minutes about what an incredible photographer I was. I never forgot that, and I took the camera and went out to get as many more pictures like it as I possibly could." He said, "Essentially, I've been doing that ever since and it goes back to that one encouraging conversation."

How many people have chosen a path in life because someone offered an encouraging word? How many young people have entered a career in athletics because at some point a father or coach said, "Wow, you are really fast. You can do it! You're incredible"? How many artists became artists when someone at a pivotal moment said, "Look at that. You really have a gift for that"? How many singers are singing today because when they were young somebody gifted them with an encouraging word? And yet I also wonder how many songs were never written, how many paintings were never painted, how many accomplishments were never achieved or dreams never even attempted because at the most vulnerable point in a person's life, instead of an encouraging word someone spoke discouragement into them. The Book of Proverbs says a cheerful word encourages a man, an encouraging word builds him up. Determine to be someone who builds others up. Try it this week. Take a day and find someone that you wouldn't ordinarily encourage and go to them and speak encouragement into his life. You can literally change someone's future.

Another way to speak constructively instead of destructively is found in this verse:

> *A gentle answer turns away wrath, but a harsh word stirs up anger.*
>
> *(Proverbs 15:1)*

The right words can solve many a problem. Gentle words can diffuse anger and prevent conflict. When someone gets angry and talks loudly you must determine to speak softly. When they talk faster you talk slower. When they speak in anger don't take it as an invitation to retaliate. Situations often become calm and problems get solved when someone speaks gently.

This is a lesson I've had to learn the hard way. I've blown this one many times but one such time I will never forget. Several years ago when I was pastoring a church in Pensacola, Florida, I went to visit the home of a lady who had been out of church for quite some time. I had only been the pastor of this church for a few months and was still getting to know its members. One of our deacons, a gentle and godly man named George, had invited me to accompany him on this visit. We arrived at the woman's home and after politely exchanging greetings she invited us to come inside and sit down. By the time we were firmly planted in our seats she began to spew her anger and resentment towards the church directly at us. Come to find out, her husband had recently passed away and, from her viewpoint, the church had failed her during his long illness. At first, I sat there and listened, trying to be patient and understanding of her deep hurt and intense bitterness. After all, she had lost her husband and I knew her grief was still very fresh and real. But she went on and on and on and on. Everything she said was just so negative and bitter.

Eventually I began to lose my patience and started thinking, "Okay, I've had about enough of this whining. This lady might be angry and disappointed in the church but I just got here. It's not my fault." At the same time, the people I had come to know in the church were wonderful and compassionate people. As I continued to listen, I grew even more irritable and impatient. I sat there waiting for her to stop talking and take a breath so I could jump in and present a defense. You see I had already quit listening. I had heard enough. I had checked out. I was already practicing the three-point sermon I was going to give her. I was going to lecture her about the importance of gratitude and the danger of a critical spirit. It was in my head, rehearsed and ready to fire. I was even ready to suggest she try another church if she thought ours was so lousy. After all, who needs another negative person around, right? I'm good at lecturing. I get paid to lecture and I was ready.

As soon as she began to wind down and take a breath I was ready to start talking. But before I could get the first syllable off of my lips, George jumped ahead of me. I couldn't believe it. What nerve he had to *minister* to this woman. I mean, wasn't I the pastor? And as far as I was concerned, there were a few things she needed to be taught. George began to speak to her with words so gentle and full of grace. He had listened patiently to her every word and responded with gentleness and compassion. The fact is, George should have been the one offended. He had been at the church for thirty years. But George seemed to know that much more was going on beneath the surface. He seemed to understand the complexity of this woman's deep grief. She had been hurt. Instead of being even slightly defensive, George said to her, "You know what? I am so sorry for your pain." Then he went on to take the full responsibility, as if the church was his alone. He said, "It's my fault. I should have been here. I have no excuse and I am very sorry. I should have called you more. I can't imagine what you've been through. I know I can't change yesterday, but I sure would like to change today and tomorrow." He asked if he could pray for her. After he prayed, he asked me if I would pray for her, too. "Yeah, I'll pray, I'll pray," I thought. I just wanted to get out of there. But do you know what? That lady came back to church the next Sunday, and for the seven years that I was pastor there, she almost never missed a service. She became a dear friend and encourager and I can honestly say that she was one of the sweetest and kindest people you could ever meet.

When I look back on that afternoon I think about how grateful I am for a spiritual man who taught me that a soft answer turns away wrath. Hurt people hurt people. We've all heard that, and it's true. Hurt people can say some harsh things, but that doesn't mean that you have to be harsh in return. If they speak in a sharp tone, you don't have to reply at the same level. If someone sends you an ugly letter it doesn't mean you must write back in the same way. Just because somebody chewed you out doesn't mean you have to engage in the banter. It is often the soft answer that has the power to diffuse a situation. There are times when tough conversations are inevitable and difficult things need to be said but if you and I can remember Proverbs 15:1 and put it into practice it will save us from a world of hurt.

Pleasant words are like a honeycomb, sweet to the soul and healing to the bones.
(Proverbs 16:24)

The tongue has the power of both life and death. The ultimate example of that truth lies in the ability of the tongue to either confess Jesus as Lord or deny Him. The Bible says:

...if you confess with your mouth that, "Jesus is Lord" and believe in your heart that God raised him from the dead, you will be saved.
(Romans 10:9)

Eternal life in heaven is the gift God gives to us when we place our faith in him. We must believe in our heart that Jesus is God's Son and accept what he did on the cross as His ransom payment for our sins. The cross was God's ultimate act of love and forgiveness. Along with believing it in your heart, you must confess it with your mouth. If you have never confessed Jesus as your Lord, I want to encourage you to put this book down and pray. Ask God to forgive you of your sins. Place your faith in Jesus and confess out loud that He is your Lord and Savior. Once you have done that, find someone to tell. Don't be ashamed to follow Him publically. He sure isn't ashamed of you. In fact, He's proud of you.

So you see, the tongue really does have the power of life and death. Your words do create worlds. The right word at the right time has the power to bring life. The wrong word at the wrong time has the power of death. So watch your words!

Letter Four

Money: Dollars and Sense

Dear Son,

Money matters. You've already noticed it matters to people. People are judged by how much they own, how much they make, and what they spend. No doubt you've already noticed that some people handle money and for some people their money handles them. Money matters a lot to people but you also need to know it matters to God. Jesus taught more about money than any single subject, more than heaven, more than hell, more than faith or love. It's not that money is more important than those things. It's just that money touches on all those things and what we do with the material realities of our life reveals our spiritual priorities.

Money reveals your personality, your priorities, and your passions. Jesus famously said that you couldn't serve both God and money. They are incompatible masters and you must choose. Will you live for money or will you live to please God? Once that choice is made the other may become your servant. Choose to live for God not money and then follow Him by making money your servant. Choose to live for a higher purpose than money. This is wise because the most valuable things in life cannot be bought or sold. Your life will primarily be defined by your relationships with God and others. There are plenty of wealthy men who can buy most anything but they can't buy the things they really need. They have a house but not a home. They can buy medicine but not peace of mind. They can afford a counselor but can't purchase a clean conscience. They can buy fine clothes but they cannot redeem a tarnished character. The things you need most in life to be happy and to live a life of significance will never be bought or sold in a store. So get your priorities right and make money your servant not your master.

Managing your money is a life skill you must learn and the sooner the better. You don't have time to lose. You either tell your money where to go or it will tell you. From the very beginning you must make a plan. It's called a budget. It means you predetermine where your money is going and what you will spend and even more importantly what you won't. Financial wisdom begins as simply as this: you must live on less than you make. Just like there are margins on a paper, you need financial margins with God and with man. The margins come from giving and saving and both are important but neither can be done without the discipline of spending less than you earn. So determine from the very beginning to give a portion away and to put a portion aside.

The biblical discipline of tithing is a time honored and God blessed practice. In the Old Testament God's people were taught to set aside the first 10% as a way of honoring God for all His blessings. I have practiced this from my earliest days and never wavered. Whether it is a dollar, a thousand, or a million, make the first step the act of honoring God by giving a portion away. That is not the end to generosity, but it surely is a helpful beginning. Then learn to save. Put some away. Whether it is a simple savings account or a more sophisticated avenue for investing, make sure you set some aside and leave it for tomorrow. It isn't faith to ignore the needs of tomorrow for the wants of today: it is foolishness and ignores God's wisdom. I suspect almost every person my age would say to someone your age that they wish they had saved more, invested more, and spent less on foolish items they didn't need and are now long gone.

Avoid debt wherever you can. Do you very best to pay for what you need now, or do without. Debt is the most common means of financial bondage. Only in the most select circumstances should you consider using debt and when you do be faithful to always pay it back. Be a man of your word in all things but especially when it comes to money. Avoid get rich quick schemes, purchases where you feel pressured to buy now or else, and if something seems too good to be true, it probably is. Gambling is just a way to lose money and greed is a cancer to the soul. Becoming a man of God means growing in wisdom about money. So worship God, love people and use money. Keep it in that order and you'll do fine.

Love,

Dad

Chapter Four
Money:
Dollars and Sense

Of what use is money in the hand of a fool, since he has no desire to get wisdom?
(Proverbs 17:16)

Show me the money! The phrase from the hit movie *Jerry Maguire* became a cultural cliché in the 1990's but it still highlights the inevitable truth that in every business deal you eventually have to talk about money. It is true in life, as well. Eventually, everyone has to have a talk about money. Success in life may not require a lot of money but it will require that you have wisdom about money. You need dollars and sense, and frankly you need more sense than dollars.

Solomon had much to say to the next generation concerning money and he definitely had the credentials to make their ears perk up. After all, Solomon was not only one of the wisest men who ever lived, but was also one of the richest. It is difficult to measure Solomon's exact net worth by today's standards but some have estimated that it would be somewhere in excess of one hundred billion dollars. He would no doubt be one of the wealthiest men alive and one of the wealthiest men who ever lived. Fortunately for you and me, he had a lot to say on the topic of money and Proverbs 17:16 is a good place to start.

> *Of what use is money in the hand of a fool, since he has no desire to get wisdom?*
> *(Proverbs 17:16)*

Solomon was saying that is does no good to give money to a foolish person. A person who has no desire to gain wisdom will not benefit from money in their hands. It will do them absolutely no good. In asking this question, Solomon is offering us a huge principle of financial health: wisdom is better than wealth.

What if I were to offer you a choice, wisdom or wealth? Which would you choose? Seriously? If I said to you, "Sign up here and I will immediately download ten million dollars into your checking account or sign over here and I will enroll you in a financial class, which would you choose? Most people would choose the immediate wealth over the wisdom. You would probably hear people say something like, "Look, I hate to be rude but if you just give me the ten million dollars I am quite certain I can figure out the rest on my own." Most people in today's society want wealth much more than they want wisdom. We see evidence of this everywhere we look. Yet, one of the wealthiest and wisest men who ever walked the earth is telling us that wealth without wisdom is a fool's choice. You see, it is far wiser to choose wisdom over wealth for numerous reasons. First of all, without wisdom wealth won't do a lot of the things that you think it will. On the contrary, it might actually do the opposite of what you want and bring you great harm. A person must have wisdom to effectively handle wealth. Secondly, if you obtain wisdom then under the right circumstances you can gain wealth. But if you have wealth without wisdom, you will likely end up losing the wealth altogether. Choose wisdom and you can have it all. Choose wealth and you just might end up with nothing. That is exactly the choice Solomon had to make.

Solomon was a young man, probably about twenty, when he became the king of Israel. His father, David, had died and the kingdom was his. That's a heavy load and a lot of responsibility for a twenty year old. Then one night God came to Solomon and made him an offer. God told him to pray for one thing, anything, and He would give it to Solomon. It sounds kind of like a "genie in a bottle" story you would see in the movies, except this really happened. God told him that He would answer any prayer of Solomon's and give him anything he could ask for. What would you ask if God put that same ballot in your lap?

Solomon made his choice that night and he asked for wisdom. Think about it: he was a twenty-year-old boy-king who could have asked for anything and he chose wisdom. That choice alone indicates that Solomon was already very wise. He was wise enough to know that what he needed more than endless money, more than limitless power, and more than enduring fame was God's wisdom. The Bible says that God was so pleased with Solomon's choice that he not only granted him wisdom but also entrusted him with great wealth and authority. Because he made the choice for wisdom, all of the other things he might have asked for he received in addition. Wisdom is the key to all other blessings in life. So Solomon says to us, "If you have to choose, choose wisdom."

Imagine a teenager who is having some serious trouble driving. He has been issued multiple speeding tickets and is continually getting into wrecks. Due to these multiple mishaps his insurance rates are skyrocketing and his parents are desperately seeking answers. Maybe you know this guy? Well, what if his parents decided the solution was to get him a faster car? Would any sane parent think that getting this teenager a NASCAR special would solve his problems? If what he wants is to go fast would the answer be to get him a faster car? Of course not! No parent is that stupid. A faster car would just create more problems. The predicament isn't that his car doesn't go fast enough but instead that he doesn't know how to handle it. Wealth is just like a really fast car. It can be a lot of fun, but it can also do a whole lot of damage. If your wealth quotient outpaces your wisdom quotient you are in for a great deal of trouble. People who think that more money will solve all of their difficulties have believed a lie. If you give a foolish person more and more money you only compound their problems. Instead, make it your goal to seek wisdom over wealth and to seek wisdom about wealth.

This generation crawls with one example after another of how wealth without wisdom only leads to disaster. Just look around. Throughout your life you will occasionally see people who come into great sums of wealth but don't necessarily have any financial wisdom. It is especially true in fields like entertainment and athletics.

Think about the high profile athletes who make millions of dollars but end up completely broke. You may be thinking that this is an exception but not the general rule. If that's what you're thinking, you're wrong. In fact, according to *Sports Illustrated*, 78% of former NFL players either go bankrupt or are in severe financial distress within two years of retiring. In the NBA, 60% of former players are broke within five years of retirement. These are young men who came into enormous sums of wealth but their wealth quotient was way over their wisdom quotient.

You see it in the lottery all the time. Since winning the lottery is based on sheer random luck and has nothing to do with wisdom or judicious choices there are countless stories of people who gain wealth without wisdom and end up with disastrous results.

Evelyn Adams won the New Jersey Lottery not once but twice. She won a total of $5.4 million. Today, all of the money is gone and she lives in a small trailer. She wrote, "Everybody wanted my money. Everybody had their hand out. I never learned one simple word in the English language, 'No.' I wish I had the chance to do it all over again."[7]

A man named William 'Bud' Post won $16.2 million in the Pennsylvania Lottery. He now lives on about $450 a month in Social Security and food stamps. He said, "I wish it had never happened. It was totally a nightmare."[8]

Suzanne Mullens won $4.2 million in the Virginia Lottery in 1993. Today she is deeply in debt to a company that lent her money using her winnings as collateral. A lawyer who is suing her said, "I understand that she has no assets."[9]

Ken Proximer was a machinist. He won one million dollars, opened a business, went bankrupt, and is now back at work as a machinist. [10]

Willie Hurt from Lansing, Pennsylvania won $3.1 million in 1989. Two years later he was broke and charged with murder. His lawyer said that he spent a fortune on a divorce and crack cocaine. [11]

Charles Riddle of Bellevue, Michigan won a one million dollar jackpot. He later got divorced and faced many lawsuits.[12] Missourian Janite Lee won $18 million in 1993, but according to published reports, eight years after winning she had filed for bankruptcy and had only seven hundred dollars left in two accounts.[13]

On and on, the stories go. The saddest one is the story of Jack Whittaker. He was a West Virginia man who was actually pretty successful in construction. Born very poor, he worked for years to build a pretty solid business. His life was good. Then on Christmas morning, 2002, he won $315 million in the Powerball Lottery. Not a bad Christmas day, right? But from that day forward his life spiraled out of control. He tried to do the right thing. He gave 15 million dollars away to two churches. His heart was in the right place and his intentions were just but the money didn't benefit his family as he had thought it would. He has been sued as many as four hundred times. People everywhere were asking him for money. The worst thing that happened was to his granddaughter who was the apple of his eye. Whittaker said,

"The greatest joy was giving her the money and watching her enjoy it." He bought her four cars and gave her a two thousand dollar a week allowance. By age eighteen she was hooked on drugs. Her boyfriend died in one of his homes under suspicious circumstances and soon after, her body was discovered as well. He says today, "Family is what makes people happy. I don't know where it'll end, but you know, I just don't like the man I've become. I don't like the hard heart I've got. I don't know who I am. I wish to God I had torn that ticket up."[14]

You say, "How can a guy make a statement like that when he won hundreds of millions of dollars?" The answer is because wealth without wisdom can do grave damage. Parents often want to leave wealth to their children when they pass on. This can be a blessing or a curse. One thing is certain: it is far better to leave your children wisdom than to leave them wealth. If you leave them wealth without wisdom, you are just putting a bad driver in a fast car. So let's get wise about wealth. Let's take a look at the wisdom Solomon passes on to the next generation about wealth.

The Limitations of Money

It is an interesting task to read through every Proverb that has something to do with money. If you do you will notice two foundational truths about wealth that can form a strong basis for your quest to become wise, and perhaps wealthy. The first bit of wisdom that Solomon would pass on is that ***you need to understand the limitations of money.***

Solomon is not naïve about money. There are some amazing things that money can do and some great things that money can buy. Solomon actually writes about some of them.

The earnings of the godly enhance their lives.
(Proverbs 10:16, NLT)

A bribe is seen as a charm by the one who gives it; they think success will come at every turn.
(Proverbs 17:8)

A gift given in secret soothes anger, and a bribe concealed in the cloak pacifies great wrath.
(Proverbs 21:14)

Yes, money can open doors. Money can purchase some nice things. It can even create incredible opportunities and there is nothing inherently wrong with any of that. It has been said, "There's nothing wrong with having the things that money can buy as long as you don't lose the things that money can't buy."

Wisdom is understanding that while money can do some things, there are other things it cannot do. Money can buy a new car or a new house and it can fund exciting trips or launch new business ventures but as it turns out, money cannot buy the most important things. Look at some of the limitations of money observed by one of the world's wealthiest men.

Do not wear yourself out to get rich; have wisdom to show restraint. Cast but a glance at riches, and they are gone, for they will surely sprout wings and fly off to the sky like an eagle.
(Proverbs 23:4-5, NLT)

A peaceful heart leads to a healthy body; jealousy s like cancer to the bones.

(Proverbs 14:30, NLT)

Riches won't help on the day of judgment, but right living can save you from death.
(Proverbs 11:4, NLT)

Better a little with the fear of the Lord, than great wealth with turmoil.
(Proverbs 15:16)

Whoever trusts in his riches will fall, but the righteous will thrive like a green leaf.
(Proverbs 11:28)

Money can't buy happiness. It can buy entertainment and amusement but it can't buy genuine happiness. Some of the world's wealthiest people are still miserable. Their relationships fail, they struggle with addictions, and they are spiritually empty. Whatever happiness you think money can buy is only temporary and will soon wear off.

Money can't buy peace of mind. There are plenty of people with lots of money that don't have peace. Peace comes from the inside not the outside. Nothing you ever buy is going to bring you lasting peace of mind.

Money can't buy security. That is what Solomon is saying when he said of money, "it sprouts wings and flies away." I heard one man say, "Money talks", and his friend replied, "Yeah, it always tells me goodbye." It can't guarantee you security. Your money is either going to leave you or you will leave it. Even if you are smart enough and fortunate enough to hang on to your money all of your life, one day you are going to leave it all.

Money can't buy peace with God. Solomon said, "It's not good in the day of judgment." Solomon is reminding us that money is a temporary asset and one day, when we stand before God, no amount of money is going to help us.

As long you understand what money can and cannot do, you are off to a good start. It can be used for temporary things but for the spiritual and eternal things of life, money is useless. It won't buy happiness, it can't produce peace of mind, it will never guarantee security, and it absolutely will not buy peace with God.

J. Paul Getty (1892-1976) was a very wealthy man with valued assets at 4 billion dollars. He wrote this in his autobiography:

> *I have never felt any envy, except for the envy I feel towards people who have the ability to make a marriage work and endure happily. It is an art I have never been able to master. My record: five marriages, five divorces, in short, five failures.*

The LA Times said he had five sons and he termed their relationship 'painful'. His most treasured offspring died at the age of twelve after a sickly life spent separated from his father. One of his grandsons was kidnapped and held for ransom. When Getty at first refused to pay they held the boy for five months and cut off his ear. One of his sons committed suicide, another lived what was described as a tortured existence, ridiculed in correspondence by his father. Here is a famously wealthy man who envies others not because they have more things but because they have the things money cannot buy.[15]

Once you understand the limitations of money then you can move on to a second bit of wisdom: *understanding how to manage money.*

The Management of Money

As I've previously stated, money is not a bad thing. I'm sure you have personally seen money do some wonderful things for people. In this life some people will always have more money than others. Several factors may determine how much money a person will have. Some of these factors are in your control and others are not. For instance, part of your earning capacity depends on your talent and ability. Some people have more talent and ability in a particular area than others. But just because someone might have more talent than you or enjoys more success than you, doesn't mean that you are of any less importance to God. Success is not the same as significance. God loves you and values you regardless of your aptitude or skill set. In His wisdom He equips us with specific capabilities, capacities and flairs. Just governments do their best to guarantee equal rights under the law but they can't guarantee equal outcomes. Some people are smarter, faster, stronger or more creative. That is just the way it is. Because of this inevitable fact there will always be some people who have more than others and earn more than others. Now this is not a free pass to ease up, slack off and not work hard. It is still your responsibility to use the gifts that God has specifically crafted in you to do the best you can in the job you have. By the same wisdom that He gifted you, you can entrust the results to Him.

Secondly, the choices you make have an economic outcome. Stephanie is a young woman who was a gifted lawyer practicing in a respected law firm who just decided that she wanted to do something else. She felt God's call to missions and is now serving in a Christian ministry that helps orphans. Her choices mean that she will now earn less than if she had continued as a lawyer and for her that's okay. I have people on my staff in our church that made a lot more money in the business world but at some point they made a choice to go into ministry. They earn less and they're okay with that. Some professions have a greater earning potential than others, but that doesn't mean that they are better for you, provide a superior quality of life or help more people. A career is just a choice you make that has a distinct economic impact. Whether a person is wise with their money or acts foolishly is also a choice with a determined economic outcome.

Finally, your context is part of your financial equation. You may believe that you are ingeniously smart and magnificently talented and could succeed anywhere. But what if you had been born into poverty in Haiti? Would you have the opportunity to become as successful? Just because you were born on third base doesn't mean you hit a triple. You may have had a family that supported you, educational conveniences, and a country with tremendous opportunities to succeed at such a high level, but others don't have those things. I'm not saying this so you will feel guilty. Just be grateful and wise. That is all God asks of you. Realize that you have been blessed by God and by other people and then do something with the blessings that you have been given.

Whether you have a little or a lot, learning how to handle money is one of the life skills you need to become a wise person. Solomon wrote a lot of things about the management of money and all of his advice on the topic can be categorized into five basic steps toward financial wisdom.

Step One: Earn It Honestly

Money reveals character. Your principles and the true seat of your affections will be revealed by how you earn and handle money. Work hard and earn money with integrity, always displaying good character. Be a person of your word and don't engage in corrupt and dishonorable practices. Value honesty and treat others with fairness and compassion. You can be assured that God is watching. Take Solomon's advice on financial integrity.

Tainted wealth has no lasting value, but right living can save your life.
(Proverbs 10:2)

The wicked man earns deceptive wages, but he who sows righteousness reaps a sure reward.
(Proverbs 11:18)

Dishonest money dwindles away, but he who gathers money little by little makes it grow.
(Proverbs 13:11)

A greedy man brings trouble to his family,...
(Proverbs 15:27)

Better a little with righteousness, than much gain with injustice.
(Proverbs 16:8)

A fortune made with a lying tongue is like a fleeting vapor and a deadly snare.
(Proverbs 21:6)

Again, earning money is a wonderful thing but if you deal dishonestly with others and compromise your integrity, your financial practices will become a trap. You may succeed in the short run but someday you will give an account to God. Solomon said that money earned through deceit is a "fleeting vapor." It won't last. Your character will last a lot longer than your money. He also called it a "deadly snare." At first it may seem fine: you may think you've gotten away with a little dishonesty or cheating but it will trap you. It leads to one bad decision after another until finally you are ensnared in a scheme that can do you in. There are plenty of people in financial ruin today, some even in jail, because they were trapped in their own lies about money. Whatever you do, whatever you earn, purpose to be this: a person who tells the truth at all costs, values others above yourself, and never compromises the integrity of your character.

Step Two: Plan It Carefully

The greatest financial mistakes that people make come from wanting to spend before they plan. First, determine what you are going to do with your money. You will either tell your money where to go or it will tell you. And you won't like where it sends you.

> *Good planning and hard work lead to prosperity.*
> *(Proverbs 21:5a)*

The key to prosperity is good planning and hard work. God does not guarantee that everyone will be wealthy but He does reveal that a failure to plan and a lazy spirit won't get you there. Solomon says:

> *...but hasty shortcuts lead to poverty.*
> *(Proverbs 21:5b)*

Another verse that emphasizes the importance of planning:

> *Be sure you know the condition of your flocks, give careful attention to your herds;*
> *(Proverbs 27:23)*

Remember, these were largely agricultural people. The people of Solomon's day did not have stocks, bonds, IRAs and bank accounts. They had herds and flocks. So what was Solomon saying? "Pay attention to your assets." He is saying, "Know the condition of your flocks. Pay attention to your herds." So why should you pay attention to those things? Why should you plan carefully?

> *Because riches do not endure forever, and a crown is not secure for all generations.*
> *(Proverbs 27:24)*

If you think that just because you have something today you will have it tomorrow, think again! Solomon had lived long enough to see people lose their wealth, to see kings die off, and dynasties overthrown. Crowns don't always endure and riches don't last forever. Therefore, you need to plan carefully.

The first step to planning well is called a budget. A budget is simply a plan you put together to determine where your money will go before you even get it. Pay attention to your flocks. Make a budget and follow it! In order to do this you must first determine how much money is coming in each month. Second, determine how much is going out and where it is going. Many people who keep an inventory for one month are surprised to see where all of their money is going. Third, set some priorities for where you want your money to go. And finally, stick to the plan! It may take a few adjustments at first but if you learn to say "no" to some things today, you will be able to say "yes" to a lot more things tomorrow. Make a plan and stick to it. Know what is coming in and what is going out and strategically plan where it goes. Make it a lifelong goal to grow in financial wisdom. Many churches offer classes on financial guidance and planning. Learn as much as you can as quickly as you can.

Step Three: Give Generously

The Bible teaches that a generous person will be blessed. One of the greatest reasons to acquire wealth is so that you can give generously and bless others. It can be one of the greatest joys in life. Generous people are almost always happy. When you meet someone who loves to give generously, they usually have a big smile and a full heart. On the contrary, I've never met a stingy person who was really happy.

In Charles Dickens' classic, *A Christmas Carol*, the infamous Ebenezer Scrooge was described as, "Hard and sharp as flint, from which no steel had ever struck out generous fire; secret, and self contained, and solitary as an oyster. The cold within him froze his old features, nipped his pointed nose, shriveled his cheek, stiffened his gait; made his eyes red, his thin lips blue; and spoke out shrewdly in his grating voice. A frosty rime was on his head, and on his eyebrows, and his wiry chin. He carried his own low temperature always about with him."[16] Does this sound like a guy you would want to hang out with? Stingy people are predominately mean, unhappy, and generally unpleasant to be around.

If one of your goals is to be a happier person one year from now, then be more generous. It's just that simple. A generous man is a blessed man.

Honor the Lord with your wealth, with the first fruits of all your crops; then your barns will be filled to overflowing, and your vats will brim over with new wine.
(Proverbs 3:9)

God doesn't only promise an emotional blessing but a financial blessing as well. You will never out give God. It's impossible. While this principle should not be twisted in an attempt to turn God into your own personal ATM machine, there is no denying the principle of planting and harvesting in the Bible. When we give to the Lord, He provides for our needs and blesses our lives. Sometimes things just last longer and don't wear out. Occasionally blessings arise from unexpected places. You might find that when you're in a crunch, things work out 'just so' and you have exactly what you need. God doesn't promise that you will get rich but He does promise to care for your needs. He always blesses the generous giver.

The Bible teaches the principle of giving away the first ten percent of your income. It is often called a tithe, meaning one-tenth. I've practiced this all of my life and can tell you that God has always been faithful. Learning the discipline of giving away the first ten percent taught me how to give, challenged me to give more, and provided a way for me to give consistently and proportionately. I have never regretted what I have given away and the older I get the more I'm thankful for that simple discipline that was built into my life at an early age. If you give God what is left over it will end up being very little. If you prioritize your giving you will give more, be blessed and discover that God will make up the difference in a multitude of ways. Make your giving the first part of your budget plan. Determine how much to give and where you will give. Commit to do this no matter how much is coming in. Then as your income grows so will your generosity.

Step Four: Save Purposefully

The next step in your budget plan should be to save. It is not faith that says, "There is no need to prepare for tomorrow," that is foolishness. Solomon says:

> *Take a lesson from the ants...learn from their ways and become wise.*
> (Proverbs 6:7, NLT)

In other words, spend some time watching an anthill one afternoon and you will learn some important lessons. You won't get any money from the ants but you will gain some wisdom.

> *Though they have no prince or governor or ruler to make them work, they labor hard all summer, gathering food for the winter.* (Proverbs 6:7, NLT)

You will observe two things from the ants: they work hard and they gather food for the winter. I've already written about the importance of hard work and we will talk about it more in a later chapter, but here the importance of saving is also emphasized. Ants continually put something away for a future season and so should you!

If you are determined to be wise with your money you will need to live on less than what comes in. Set some aside to give and some aside to save. Many financial counselors advise that you give ten percent away, save ten percent, and live off the rest. When it comes to saving (and giving), the sooner you start the better. Don't wait until you think you are making a lot of money, and don't wait until you have 'extra' because that day will almost certainly never come. Start right now! Start with what you have. The habit is more important than the amount.

To illustrate how important it is to begin saving early, I asked a financial advisor to do some basic calculations.

If you are 30 years of age and you decide to put $2,000 a year away and it gains 7% interest a year for 35 years, at age 65 you would have $276,473. Not bad. Not bad for putting only $2,000 away in something that earns at least 7% interest per year. But watch this: If you had started sooner, say 18, and put the same amount away, by the time you were 65 it would have grown to $658,448. That is almost $400,000 more just because you started earlier.

Develop the habit of saving and start right now. Don't spend every penny you make. Plan in advance what to do with it. Give the first part away and save the next part. Then, with what is left…

Step Five: Spend It Wisely

It won't surprise you that Solomon also has a lot to say about spending wisely. He warns us about many of the most common financial mistakes people make.

> *An inheritance claimed too soon will not be blessed at the end.*
> *(Proverbs 20:21)*

> *It's poor judgment to guarantee another person's debt or put up security for a friend.*
> *(Proverbs 17:18, NLT)*

> *Don't agree to guarantee another person's debt or put up security for someone else. If you can't pay it, even your bed will be snatched from under you.*
> *(Proverbs 22:26-27, NLT)*

Avoid get-rich-quick schemes and borrowing money. These schemes are usually traps designed by someone who wants to separate you from your money. People will be getting rich all right but it won't be you! Avoid hasty decisions. If in doubt take time to pray about it and get good counsel. Avoid getting trapped by co-signing a loan for someone else or signing up for something you haven't spent time researching and praying about. When someone pushes you to make a decision "right now," hit the pause button and back up. A good deal today will usually be there tomorrow. A hasty decision today can cost you dearly tomorrow.

Most people have made some kind of financial mistakes in their life. I often encourage young people to ask their parents or a mentor about their worst financial mistake. They are usually happy to relate the event and it almost always involves a hasty decision or irresponsible borrowing. More often than not it involves both! The quickest way to get in financial trouble is through borrowing. Borrowing is using tomorrow's money for today's pleasure. Solomon offers serious warnings about borrowing.

> *Just as the rich rule the poor, the borrower is servant to the lender.*
> *(Proverbs 22:7)*

Solomon doesn't condemn every form of borrowing and this shouldn't be taken as an absolute prohibition against using credit. What he does say is that there is a principle in life that a borrower is always a servant to their lender. If you have ever borrowed money you know this is true. If you borrow from a bank, the bank gets to tell you what to do. They can even go so far as telling you how you must administer your business. After all you owe them and at least in some part of your life they are now in charge.

Financial pressure is also one of the most common factors in marital strife. When marriages fail people usually cite financial burdens as one of the biggest contributing factors and debt is the primary cause of that burden.

Borrowing will make everything cost more, add stress to your life, and put you in financial danger tomorrow. Too many people are spending their money today to pay for things they bought yesterday and have already forgotten. If they are paying interest then the hole just gets deeper and deeper. Yes, there are legitimate reasons for borrowing. It can be done with wisdom and prudence but the wise person avoids it whenever they can. The wise person uses credit cards with extreme discretion and always pays the balance at the end of the month. Make it your goal to never carry a balance on a credit card. Never pay interest to a bank for items you have already bought and are declining in value.

Of course there will be exceptions. Unusually large items like a car or a house are major purchases that usually require some level of borrowing. A house can be a good investment and appreciate over time but cars seldom do. Cars quickly lose their value and are rarely good investments. Yes, there are emergency situations but those should be rare exceptions. If you go out and start buying entertainment, food, clothes, and gas on credit and don't budget to pay for them right away you will quickly get into a financial hole that creates stress and bondage in your life.

When payday finally comes, after you've planned, given and saved, make sure you meet your debts and obligations first. Try to pay off your debts and don't add any more. There will always be obligations such as insurance, a mortgage or rent and other bills to pay so make sure you first take care of the things to which you have already committed.

After you have planned, saved, given and met your obligations, you are free to enjoy your money. True, there might only be a little left over, and maybe in the beginning none at all. But if you stay out of debt, work hard, live wisely, keep saving and giving, your income will grow over time. Then you may enjoy it without added stress in your life and you won't be adding debt that will make tomorrow harder. Now that is really enjoying your money! Is it really enjoyment when you do something today that creates guilt and bondage tomorrow?

If you want to grow wise, you must learn how to handle money. You must learn its limitations. You must realize that there are many important things money cannot do. Once you accept its limitations, you can make it your servant and not your master. Your life will never be defined by the amount of things you own. Then learn to handle it wisely. Work, plan, save, give and spend. Do it in that order and do it with wisdom. Then you'll grow rich in the things that matter most.

Letter Five
Relationships: Friends, Foes & Fools

Dear Son,

Watch out for crowds. It isn't so much that I don't like big events. I do. I love people. Crowds can be fun. Crowds can be enthusiastic. Crowds can have a contagious influence which is why you need to watch out for them. When it comes to determining the direction of your life, following the crowd is about the worst thing you can do. The crowd is almost always headed in the wrong direction.

Truth is never determined by an opinion poll and God's blessing doesn't come from a majority vote. In the Bible most of the time they took a vote the majority got it wrong. Just asked the Israelites who wandered for 40 years in the wilderness and lost a generation because they decided to follow the majority.

Choose your relationships carefully because they will define you and mark the course of your life. Every relationship is also a choice and every choice is setting your course. You are foolish if you believe that others will not influence you. We are all influenced by other people. So when you choose whom you walk with, whom you listen to, and whom you laugh with, be careful. Who you hang with determines where you are headed and where you are headed determines where you will end up. There are people in jail today, because they choose the wrong friends. Others are addicted, divorced, embittered, broke, violated, and full of rage because way back when they chose a friend or a group of friends that ended up taking them where they never thought they would go. There are people in hell today because they chose the wrong friends.

You will become more and more like the people you hang with and listen to. This will happen whether you want it to or not. This will happen whether you think it will or not. So choose wisely. Walk with the wise and become wise. Walk with fools and suffer the consequences.

Life is all about relationships. You will meet all kinds of people. Love them. Be friendly to all but choose your friends carefully. Be compassionate to all but be careful about who become your companions. In life there are friends, foes and fools. It pays to know the difference.

With adversaries learn to be compassionate. The first rule of fights is don't get in one. A hot-tempered man is to be avoided. Look to solve problems not cause them. When you do face adversaries and critics learn to be a person of character and compassion. When they stumble don't gloat over their fall. When they have a need be the first one to step forward and offer a hand. Always be willing to take a step toward peace and reconciliation. Don't hold grudges. Forgive your enemies and pray for them. God will use your critics and adversaries to build your character.

Watch out for fools. There are those who ignore the wisdom of the ages and who discount the truth of God. They will call good evil and evil good. There are those who laugh at God and mock spiritual things. There are those who rush headlong into immorality, irresponsibility, and decadent living. You will do well to stay away, far away. A companion of fools suffers harm so stay clear.

Find the wise and make them your friends. Listen and learn and never stop doing either. Remember sometimes friends have to tell you the hard stuff and sometimes you have to return the favor. Find those who are wise. Find those who will speak the truth whether it is popular or not. Find those who are following after Christ. Determine to be a friend of the wise and you will grow wise indeed.

Love,

Dad

Chapter Five

Relationships: Friends, Foes and Fools[17]

He who walks with the wise grows wise, but a companion of fools suffers harm.
(Proverbs 13:20)

We've all heard it and every parent has said it, "Be careful who you hang around." Bad company corrupts good morals. I wonder how many times I've heard a parent say, "I don't know what happened? My child was doing just fine and his attitude was great and then all of a sudden they started hanging around the wrong crowd and the next thing I knew they were making terrible choices."

Such reasoning can never absolve a person of their responsibilities or their choices, but there is something very true about the power of influence. There is something tragically true about the corrupting power of negative influences. That is why we read the following words from a father to his son, words that are simple yet hold the power to alter a life.

> *He who walks with the wise grows wise, but a companion of fools suffers harm.*
> *(Proverbs 13:20)*

A person who walks with wise company isn't just wise, but they grow wiser and wiser as time passes. Conversely, a person who surrounds himself with fools will inevitably suffer harm and make bad choices. The company you choose to keep will determine where your life will go. The people with whom you spend your time will determine the direction your future will take. Your destiny can often be predicted by taking a good look at whom you surround yourself with today.

Who are you walking with? Who are your companions? Who are you reading? Who are you listening to? Who are you spending time with? If you want to grow wise you must walk with wise people.

Now some may consider this verse harsh. After all, aren't we supposed to be kind to everyone? Aren't we supposed to intentionally build relationships with people far from God in order to influence them for good? Absolutely! But there is a difference between being friendly and being a close friend. There is a large ravine between a casual friendship and a deep partnership. When Solomon talks about walking with the wise he is talking about an alliance. He is talking about a key, lasting relationship, a close consort or companion. The prophet Amos asked, *Do two walk together unless they have agreed to do so?* (Amos 3:3, NIV) There is something going on when you see two people walking together. You know they have a relationship and have decided to head in the same direction. So, who is it that you are you walking with?

If you walk with the wise, you get wiser. If you are a companion of fools, you will end up suffering harm. Whom you hang out with determines where you are heading. It's as simple as that.

The Principle of Influence

People influence one another. Sometimes an influence is good and other times it's bad. One thing is for certain though: whom you spend your time with is influencing you whether you see it or not. You are either growing wiser, or getting more foolish. Sometimes we lie to ourselves. We don't want to believe that the people we associate with have a direct influence over us. We convince ourselves that we are influencing *them* and so it's okay. For instance, maybe some friends needed a designated driver and you were the nice guy that volunteered to help. Now you're hanging out weekend after weekend with drunk people. You see, here's the deal. You *might* be influencing them. In fact, maybe you're having some good influence on them, and that's a great thing in its place. But this I can guarantee you: they are also influencing you. They are guiding your life more than you realize and in the end you could be sacrificing the very influence you intended to have on them. If you want to take your life in the right direction, you better surround yourself with the right people who want to get you there. There are no exceptions. The person who walks with wise people gets wiser and wiser. The company you keep determines the course you take. Whom you fraternize with today will affect what your life is going to look like 10, 20 or even 30 years from now. Take a good look around you. What do you think?

Several years ago I heard John Calipari, the men's basketball coach at the University of Kentucky, explain his decision to release a young man from his team. This particular kid had a bad attitude and the coach saw that attitude poison the entire team. Coach Calipari was a championship coach, and he knew a thing or two about leadership and influence. He sat the young man down a tried to give him a picture about the power of influence. He said, "It's like I've got a bucket of ice cream. I've got this bucket of delicious homemade ice cream. Then over here on the other side of the table I've got another bucket—of horse manure. It's just stinky, steamy, just yuck. So there's a bucket of horse manure and there's a bucket of ice cream. Now, son, let me explain something to you. I can take as much ice cream as I want and put it into a bucket of horse manure. I can take huge spoonfuls of it. I can take cups of it, and just keep putting the ice cream into the bucket of horse manure and stir it around and it doesn't make the horse manure any better. It's still awful. Nobody will eat it. It doesn't matter how much ice cream you pour into the horse manure, it's still horse manure and you don't want any of it. No amount of ice cream will make the manure edible."

He continued, "But what if instead I take a very small spoonful of manure and put it in the ice cream bucket? I take just a small amount of manure and put it in the ice cream and stir it around. Guess what? No matter how small the spoonful of manure, it ruins the whole batch of ice cream."

Then he asked, "Son, do you understand that?" The young man nodded his head and replied with a yes. Then the coach remarked, "Son, you are the manure in our ice cream."

That is the power of influence: a little bit of bad can corrupt a lot of good. You can lie and tell yourself that you will be a good influence on others, but the truth is that if you become a companion of fools, you're actually sacrificing influence. Any influence you might have on them will be trumped by the influence they will have on you.

Through the years I have noticed that a person's spiritual growth can often be charted back to a certain point where they made a decision to sever a specific relationship in their life. This may be true with you. You might have relationships that need a severe boundary in order for you to move ahead with God. Proverbs is telling us that there are people you just can't walk with. In some cases you might be thinking, "But this is a person I love!" I understand that dilemma. It's okay to love a fool, but if you choose to walk with one you will suffer harm. It's impossible to grow in wisdom if you choose not to surround yourself, listen to, laugh with, and run the race of life alongside people who are wise. Tell me where you're hanging, and I'll tell you where you're headed. Tell me whom you're walking with, and I'll tell you where that path leads. This is the principle of influence.

The Principle of Direction

The second thing you need to understand to fully appreciate this Proverb is the principle of direction. We've already nailed down the truth that those who walk with the wise grow wiser. It is also important to note that the wisdom you gain takes you in a specific direction. You see, there is another very simple but profound truth we must note. You are going to end up wherever you're headed. That sentence seems self-evident, but it is a fact that is often overlooked. If you walk with the wise you end up not only wiser, but headed in a direction that wisdom takes you. If you walk with fools, you not only suffer harm, but will one day look around and wonder how you got to where you didn't want to go. Think about it. You will eventually end up wherever it is you're headed.

I live in the beautiful oasis known as the Tampa Bay area. It's about halfway down the coast of Florida's western peninsula. Interstate 75 runs north and south directly through our town. If you take this interstate south and travel for four hours you will end up in Miami. If you drive it north you're going to hit Atlanta about eight hours later. Of course, the direction you take will depend on where you want to end up. That's logical, right? So, let's say that you come to me and say, "I need to get out of town for a few days. I want to end up near the sand, blue water and palm trees of Miami Beach." Great! I would tell you to head east out of town, find I-75 and then travel south. Continue south and you will eventually run into Miami Beach.

But let's say you start your trip, and although in your mind you want to end up in Miami Beach, you happen to be driving with people who don't want to go south. They want to go north. They don't want to go all the way to Atlanta, they just happen to have time to kill and want to head north for a while. So, you find yourself thinking, "Well, what's the harm? I still want to go to Miami Beach, but I don't mind going north on I-75 for a little while. I'm still going to get to Miami Beach."

So you drive north out of town, all the while laughing and having fun with your friends. For a time it's no big deal at all. The drive north doesn't look much different than what you imagine the drive south would look like. Besides, you're hanging with your buds and who likes to travel alone anyway? You might even find yourself laughing at all of the people who told you that if you went north you'd end up in Atlanta. I mean, it's been an hour and you haven't seen anything that looks like Atlanta. At this point you're cruising by a cow pasture giggling to yourself at how little your mother knows about where this road north really leads. I mean, she said you would end up in Atlanta! What does she know?

As you continue for a couple more hours your mind begins to wander. Time is passing and you're thinking, "I'm not even in Georgia. What does my pastor know? He always warned us that if we headed north on I-75 we'd end up in Atlanta. What a loser! He doesn't know anything. We're just hanging out, having a great time and we're not hurting anybody." Time continues to pass and you think, "We're still not in Atlanta!" Soon you doze off and someone else begins to drive. When you wake up and look around, guess where you find yourself? Yep. You're stuck in the traffic of downtown Atlanta. Do you know what happens next? Maybe you've been here. Maybe you pick up your cell phone and ask someone, "How could this happen? How could God let this happen to me?" To make matters worse, you just figured out that Miami Beach is much farther away now than it was when you started. "There weren't enough signs! I drove for hours and didn't see anything even close to Atlanta!" It's easy to blame your destination on many factors, but the truth is, it's no one's fault but yours. You made the choice. You went in one direction and that's why you ended up where you did.

If you think that story is farfetched let me assure you that I hear stories like this all the time. Just like the destination of Miami Beach, people have big dreams and goals for their lives. They want healthy relationships, financial security, a great family, and emotional happiness. Many have an idea of what they want and even have clear directions on how to get there (the Bible). But they still get on the interstate going the wrong direction. For a time, it doesn't seem to matter much. Some of them even scoff at the warnings that people gave them with statements like, "Hey, it's just college," "I'm still in my twenties; now is the time to live a little" or "I'll only be single for a while, I may as well have some fun now." And with those words they merge onto the interstate of life, persuaded by the current of the loud and rapidly moving traffic, until one day they realize that in the rush of those crowds, they have been swept many miles in the wrong direction.

Maybe you've woken up at thirty or forty years of age wondering what happened to that dream of a healthy marriage or a great career. Maybe you've stood face to face with the reality that you're up to your eyeballs in debt. Maybe the road you've chosen has led you to a place where you're asking questions like, "How did I get here?" or "How could God let this happen to me?" But, the truth is, God didn't have anything to do with it. You took the turn and you went down the road, and ten years later you've ended up exactly where you were heading. You may have thought that you were just making a choice, but you weren't, you were setting a course. You see, you aren't just making a decision, you're choosing a destination.

Every choice you make contributes to the course you set for your life. One key ingredient you may not have considered is time. Time is the great arbitrator between the decision and the destination, and with time the destination always wins. It's the principal of the path. You're going to end up where you're heading so you've got to move in the right direction. The person who is wise and walks with the wise gets wiser and wiser. The person who is a companion of fools will suffer harm. You're not just making a decision, you're choosing a direction. That chosen direction combined with a heaping spoonful of time will inevitably result in a predicted destination.

If you go off to college believing that *"It's just college,"* then you're sorely mistaken. Four years of actively pointing your life's compass in a specific direction is going to take you somewhere. You might be thinking, *"But they're just friends."* There's no "just" about it. They're companions that you have chosen, and they're walking with you in a direction that you have set. You better make sure it's where you want to go.

I talked to a guy one time that lived with great regret. Fortunately for him, he made a U-turn in the right direction before he got too far down a dangerous path. He told me, "I can trace the time I walked away from God back to a single choice during my freshman year of college." He had been very active in his church's high school ministry and a leader in their dynamic youth group. God had taken him to deep places spiritually, and when he left for college he was on fire for the Lord. Here was a guy who loved God, believed in God and wanted to live his life for God. But he told me that he could trace his journey away from the Lord back to a single moment and a single decision in a college dorm.

After only a few weeks away at school he got lonely. He didn't know a soul on campus and hadn't been able to connect with any particular student group, club or ministry yet. One day, as he walked out the door to his room, he saw that another dorm room door was open. Inside he was greeted by a handful of guys who offered him a beer and a place to hang out. Feeding into his loneliness and isolation in a new environment, he made a decision that he had no idea would spiral him into months of running from God. You see, that one beer became two and two became twelve and the downward spiral accelerated. He traced what he referred to as a nightmare back to one specific choice. Fortunately, he turned to God and God rescued him from a deep pit that he himself had dug.

Another man shared how he traced his financial collapse and bankruptcy back to one decision to a buy a lottery ticket. What seemed like an innocent diversion turned into a lifelong gambling addiction that cost him everything. One single choice has the power to mark the course of your life. One single decision can set the direction that will determine your destiny.

There's a third principle that helps bring understanding to this verse.

The Principle of Discernment

The principle of discernment is this: If you are going to make any of these principles work in your life, you have got to be able to discern the wise from the foolish. If you're going to choose to walk with wise people and avoid walking with foolish people, you are going to have to know the difference. In order to do that you must practice discernment. Now, this can be tricky because if there is one thing people don't want to be, it's *judgmental.* In today's world if you tell someone they are wrong, they're likely to ask, "Who are you to judge me?" We don't like being around judgmental people and we definitely don't want to be one. In fact, the most quoted verse in the Bible is *Judge not, that you be not judged (Matthew 7:1).* It is also one of the most misused and misunderstood verses, as well. Jesus is warning about having a judgmental spirit. There is a difference between practicing good judgment and being judgmental. A judgmental person is one that minimizes their own faults and maximizes the faults of someone else. Using good judgment, on the other hand, is a quality of being wise.

In Matthew 7 Jesus talks about a guy who has a beam (something huge) in his own eye and doesn't see it, but instead looks at the speck in someone else's eye.

This parable paints the picture of a man who minimizes his own problems and maximizes everyone else's. We all know people like this, and we don't want to be this way. But there is a world of difference between being judgmental and practicing good judgment. When someone comes along and says, "Well, I don't want to be judgmental" all the while refusing to practice good judgment, he will never know the wise from the fools and is a fool himself. Refusing to practice good judgment will make you a companion of fools, and you will suffer harm.

Now the truth is, good judgment is necessary and, believe it or not, judging others is, too. If you're honest you know it, and you do it. Let's say you're looking for a babysitter for Friday night. A friend of yours mentions this guy who just moved in a few blocks away from you. He recently got out of jail after serving a sentence for child abuse and works really cheaply. Your friend also tells you that she doesn't think he was actually released from jail. It's possible that he just broke out, but he's available Friday night. Well, are you going to practice some judgment? You better or you're an unfit parent!

Say a guy comes to you knowing that you're looking for an accountant for your business. He says he knows just the guy and hands you his resume. On the resume the would-be accountant lists that he just beat a rap on forgery and has filed for bankruptcy three times. You proceed to look back up at your friend who is telling you that fortunately the guy is available and would love to work with your checkbook. Are you going to practice good judgment or are you going to worry about someone accusing you of being judgmental? If you don't practice good judgment then you're an unfit businessperson. It is critical to practice good judgment in parenting, in business and in life. I'm not talking about maximizing the faults of others and minimizing your own. I'm talking about practicing good judgment.

Pastor James Merritt wrote a book on Proverbs entitled *Friends, Foes & Fools* where he offers some great advice on how to handle all three.[18] Before you can decide how to handle them, you must use good judgment to tell the difference between the three. So how do you handle foes? Friends? How about fools?

How do you handle foes?

Be compassionate with foes. There will always be critics in your life. There will always be people around you that are competitors. As Christians, we must show kindness to our adversaries. The Bible tell us:

> *If your enemy is hungry, give him food to eat; if he is thirsty, give him water to drink.*
> *(Proverbs 25:21)*

This doesn't mean that we should give everybody we meet anything they want. It means that when someone has a legitimate need that I am capable to meet, even if they are my critic, my adversary, or my competitor, I should be the first one to meet that need. Here's another verse on how to handle foes:

> *Starting a quarrel is like breaching a dam; so drop the matter before a dispute breaks out.*
> *(Proverbs 17:14)*

Do you know what happens when a dam is breached? When water continues to rise behind a dam and reaches the top, that water will start to rush over the edge with impressive force that is impossible to stop. You see, just like the power of a rushing waterfall produced by an unrestrained current, so are the difficulties ensued by trying to finish a fight that could have been avoided. Fights are much easier to start than they are to finish. The first rule of fights is not to get in one. If you can possibly avoid it stay out of it.

> *Do not gloat when your enemy falls; when they stumble, do not let your heart rejoice, or the Lord will see and disapprove and turn his wrath away from them.*
> *(Proverbs 24:17-18)*

Finally, when your enemy stumbles and falls, don't be arrogant. Don't rejoice over their demise. Show character. Be compassionate with your foes.

How do you handle fools?

Proverbs warns us to be cautious with fools. You're going to run into some fools here and there and the Bible warns us to tread carefully. In fact, what it's really saying is to stay away from them. If you want to grow in your walk with God there are some relationships that might have to be relinquished. The Bible says:

Stay away from foolish man, for you will not find knowledge on his lips.
(Proverbs 14:7)

Do not envy wicked men, do not desire their company;
(Proverbs 24:1)

Over and over in Proverbs we are warned to stay away from those who are foolish. If you gather together all of the proverbs that describe a fool you will find three distinct categories. Each of these should be a warning sign to us to use discernment.

First, a fool ignores godly counsel. When you deliver wisdom to a fool they become argumentative and defensive. They don't listen to outside advice because they think they know it all. Listen to these proverbs:

For lack of guidance a nation falls, but victory is won through many advisers.
(Proverbs 11:14)

Plans fail for lack of counsel, but with many advisors they succeed.
(Proverbs 15:22)

...let the wise listen and add to their learning, and let the discerning get guidance—
(Proverbs 1:5)

Notice that a wise person is always seeking to add to their knowledge and never thinks they've learned enough. They want more. Although already discerning, a wise person still seeks guidance.

Pride only breeds quarrels, but wisdom is found in those who take advice.
(Proverbs 13:10)

Listen to advice and accept instruction, and in the end you will be wise.
(Proverbs 19:20)

The way of a fool seems right to him, but a wise man listens to advice.
(Proverbs 12:15)

Solomon, the wisest man who ever lived, emphasizes the importance of allowing other wise people to speak into your life. Who are the wise people that you allow to speak direction into your life? Who are your counselors? Who speaks truth into your life about marriage, finances, parenting and spiritual life? Do you have people that are free to speak wisdom into your life? Do you listen?

Secondly, a fool is hot tempered. Have you ever known someone who seems mad about everything? I know some people whom I agree with about a lot of things, but because they are hot-tempered and easily angered I stay away. I might agree with them on some issues, but because of their tendency to get mad and worked up I find it best to stay at arms-length. The Bible says to watch out for a hot-tempered man.

A hot-tempered man stirs up dissensions, but a patient man calms a quarrel.
(Proverbs 15:18)

It is to a man's honor to avoid strife, but every fool is quick to quarrel.
(Proverbs 20:3)

Drive out the mocker, and out goes strife; quarrels and insults are ended.
(Proverbs 22:10)

Leaders will tell you that if there are problems within their organization it can often be traced back to one person who is stirring up strife and dissension. Oftentimes, if you get rid of the right person the strife leaves with them. Drive out the mocker, and out goes the strife.

Do not make friends with a hot-tempered man, do not associate with one easily angered, or you may learn his ways and get yourself ensnared.
(Proverbs 22:24)

As charcoal to embers and as wood to fire, so is a quarrelsome man for kindling strife.
(Proverbs 26:21)

An angry man stirs up dissension, and a hot-tempered one commits many sins.
(Proverbs 29:22)

He who loves a quarrel loves sin; he who builds a high gate loves destruction.
(Proverbs 17:19)

Do you know what it means to build a high gate? A high gate is a person who says, "I don't want to listen. Don't tell me what to do." A high gate is a person who walls themselves off from others. A high gate invites destruction.

A hot-tempered man must pay the penalty; if you rescue him you will have to do it again.
(Proverbs 19:19)

A man who can't control himself will get in trouble. The Bible warns that if you rescue him, you will have to do it again. If you bail him out, you haven't helped him at all. You're just sending yourself an invitation to do it over and over again.

Thirdly, a fool pursues evil. A fool doesn't care about moral boundaries or absolute standards. He chases after evil. Proverbs 4 says:

Don't do as the wicked do, and don't follow the path of evildoers. Don't even think about it; don't go that way. Turn away and keep moving. For evil people can't sleep until they've done their evil deed for the day. They can't rest until they've caused someone to stumble. They eat the food of wickedness and drink the wine of violence!
(Proverbs 14:9)

Fear the Lord and the king, my son, and do not join with the rebellious,
(Proverbs 24:21)

A fool finds pleasure in evil conduct, but a man of understanding delights in wisdom.
(Proverbs 10:23)

Fools make fun of guilt, but the godly acknowledge it and seek reconciliation.
(Proverbs 14:9)

Be on the lookout. Fools pursue evil, they're hot-tempered and they ignore counsel. They're not whom you want to be walking with.

How do you handle friends?

Be committed to friends. If God has given you wise people to walk closely with in your life, commit to them. They are a treasure that can be hard to find.

A man of many companions may come to ruin, but there is a friend who sticks closer than a brother.
(Proverbs 18:24)

Look closely at that verse. Solomon is saying that a guy can have too many "friends." He is warning us of the danger in having so many friends that none of them could be considered close. Many people measure their self-worth by the number of friends they claim on Facebook or the number of followers they have on Twitter. Social media friends are not true friends. A true friend is someone who is there when you really need them, someone whose heartstrings have been tied to you in such a way that they hurt when you hurt and rejoice when you rejoice. What you want is a friend that will stick closer than a brother.

A friend loves at all times, and a brother is born for adversity.
(Proverbs 17:17)

James Merritt writes, "A friend is one who will walk in the front door when everybody is walking out the back door." [19] That's the kind of friend you want. That's the kind of friend we all need.

As iron sharpen iron, so one man sharpens another.
(Proverbs 27:17)

There are two root qualities that must be present in a close friendship.

First, you need a friend who is truthful. You need someone in your life that will love you enough to always tell you the truth. You need someone who will come to you without arrogance or anger, and who loves you enough to be willing to speak truth into your situations and decisions.

He who listens to a life-giving rebuke will be at home among the wise.
(Proverbs 15:31)

The Bible says that a wise man listens to reproof. If you have a friend who is mature enough to know the truth and loves you enough to share it, and if you are wise enough to hear it and thankful to receive it, you have a friendship worth more than the most valuable of treasures.

You also need a friend who is faithful. When God blesses you with true and treasured friends, you must be a faithful friend in return.

Do not forsake your friend or a friend of your family,
(Proverbs 27:10)

There are going to be friends, foes and fools in this world, and it's imperative that you know the difference. Your decisions concerning whom you hang around will determine where your life is heading. You tell me who you spend your Friday nights with and I'll tell you where you're going to be in twenty years. It's that easy. No, I don't have a crystal ball, but I don't need one. Just show me who you're doing life with, who you're laughing with, and who you're spending your time with. I can take a good look at their lives and their choices and give you a glimpse of where you're going to land. Who you choose to hang with will determine where you're headed and where you're headed is where you're going to end up.

Letter Six

Sex:
Love, Lust & Everything In-Between

❖

Dear Son,

As you begin your journey into manhood there is one decision you will make that will determine more than all the others. With the single exception of your commitment to Christ, this decision more than any will affect your future happiness and effectiveness. It will have ramifications that are spiritual and eternal. I speak of whom and how you will love.

God's design has been made clear from the beginning. It is clear even from natural observation. When God made the first man he saw that he was incomplete and created a companion, a woman. God declared His purpose when in the opening verses of the Bible He purposed that it was His design for a man and woman to leave their father and mother, to commit themselves exclusively to one another and that the two would become in some mystical, glorious way, one flesh. So this is where sex, love and marriage come into play. God has designed this so that one day you can become one with a companion and know an intimacy that cannot be found in any other relationship. It will be a relationship not unlike the one God desires to have with us. That is the purpose of sex and of marriage: to know and be known. Fully. Completely. And if in the course of this life you know and share a love like that, you are blessed indeed.

There are of course people who God has specifically gifted to live as singles. Our Lord never married. Paul, the great apostle was single and spoke of some advantages that brings. It is a totally legitimate and, for those so chosen, blessed way to live. But, at least for now, I will assume that for you there will come a day when you find love and weigh the choice of committing yourself wholly to one woman for all of your life. If that is to be so, it is a matter of vital importance that you prepare for that day. It is important that every relationship and moral choice you make keeps the day in mind when you will give yourself to another. Make sure the story you tell that day is one you want to tell. Live in such a way that when that day comes there will be no regrets.

Nothing is so challenging and, in today's culture, so confusing. We live in a time when men believe moral truth is determined by an opinion poll or a political election. This is deception at its greatest because the stakes, when it comes to love, are so very high. The truth is, what God has purposed from the beginning is that one man and one woman should be committed to one another. I wish this for you. I pray this for you. I know what it is to be loved unconditionally. I cannot imagine this journey through life without the intimate, faithful love of one woman.

Determine from the beginning to be a one-woman man. Guard your heart and mind because there will be no greater battle than the one which invites moral and sexual compromise. It will require a deep commitment and consistent effort to remain morally pure waiting the day of intimacy. You may even be criticized and maligned for such a commitment. But remember, it is no sacrifice to give up something today to receive something greater tomorrow. It is an investment. Every decision you make for purity is an investment in an intimate relationship tomorrow. Purity is the pathway to intimacy. The bride you may one day receive deserves your faithfulness even now. She will be worth it. The intimacy you can enjoy for a lifetime with her is worth whatever price must be paid today.

When that day comes, when you take a wife as your companion, there will be much more to learn. But for now, live for that day. Treat all women with purity and respect. Guard your heart, your eyes and your mind. And one day, if God is so graciously inclined, He may give you a bride to take for your own. To love, cherish, and honor. What you choose today may well determine whether you are ready then. So walk wisely and one day you will love deeply.

Love,

Dad

Chapter Six

Sex: Love, Lust & Everything In-between

❖

May your fountain be blessed, and may you rejoice in the wife of your youth. A loving doe, a graceful deer—may her breasts satisfy you always, may you ever be intoxicated with her love. Why, my son, be intoxicated with another man's wife? Why embrace the bosom of a wayward woman?
(Proverbs 5:18-20)

Sex can be the most awkward thing to talk about, especially when it is a conversation between parents and their kids. Overwhelmingly, parents say too little, too late. If you have a parent or older mentor who has tried to have a conversation with you about sexual issues, be thankful. Cut them some slack if it seemed awkward, or if you think it wasn't enough information, or even too much! At least they tried, and since everyone carries baggage, just making the effort is an act of enormous love and an investment into your life. If not, well there are still ways to learn some critical truths about sex.

Fortunately for all of us, Solomon included sex as one of the topics he chose to address. In fact, it is a major theme in the book of Proverbs, and that is a good thing because it is one of the major battlegrounds in life.

Sexual standards in our culture have changed through the years, and more and more people simply embrace an "anything goes" approach. After all "its just sex" isn't it? Ideas seem to be constantly modulating with the trend of the culture, but God's truth never does. It may surprise you, but there is nothing about sex that's really new. The temptations and the struggles are the same today as they have always been, it's only the delivery systems that have changed.

So it's no surprise that one of the wisest men who ever lived would spend some time talking about sex. After all, if you're going to pass along wisdom to the next generation, you have to address one of the most mysterious, complex and powerful issues in all of our lives.

Some of the longest sections in the book of Proverbs are devoted to sex. Solomon writes about morals, temptation and how to live according to God's design. In chapters 5-7, Solomon's main topic is sex. He talks about what you need to avoid and what you should embrace. In the midst of the discussion in chapter 5, Solomon summarizes some powerful truths about sex in verses 15-20.

> *Drink water from your own cistern, running water from your own well. Should your springs overflow in the streets, your streams of water in the public squares? Let them be yours alone, never to be shared with strangers. May your fountain be blessed, and may you rejoice in the wife of your youth. A loving doe, a graceful deer— may her breasts satisfy you always, may you ever be intoxicated with her love. Why, my son, be intoxicated with another man's wife? Why embrace the bosom of a wayward woman?*
> *(Proverbs 5:15-20)*

Throughout this section the concept of "water" is a metaphor for our sexuality. Solomon uses words like water, well, springs and streams. He is telling us how to find sexual fulfillment and how to avoid disaster. Just as sex can bring you great pleasure, it can also bring great pain. How you handle this area of your life can be the difference between happiness and grief, healthy relationships or broken ones, even life and death.

Sex is like water in many ways. In the mid-90's, I had the opportunity to visit the small town of Alton, Illinois. I toured the downtown area of the city where Abraham Lincoln and Stephen Douglas had once engaged in one of their great debates, but what I remember the most about that trip was the extensive damage that had been caused by the great flood of 1993. That year record floods devastated small towns up and down the Mississippi River. A few years later you could still see the damage. Dark watermarks on high walls caught my eyes, some even traced by paint to show where the water had crested. Buildings and stores still lay empty, damaged beyond repair and never reopened. I thought then about something I've seen many times now since: good things can become bad things when they spill over their boundaries.

A river is a good thing. Cities spring up along its banks and people enjoy its beauty, but when a good thing overflows its banks, it quickly becomes a bad thing. Sex is like that. It is a good thing, a God-created thing, but when that which God has made for our good gets outside the boundaries designed by God Himself, it quickly becomes a destructive force in our lives.

There is another very important concept about sex in these verses: it is highly addictive. Notice a very important word that is used twice in this passage, once in verse 19 and a second time in verse 20. In the NIV it is translated "intoxicated."

> *...be <u>intoxicated</u> with her love* *(Proverbs 5:19)...*
> *Why...be <u>intoxicated</u> with another man's wife?*
> *(Proverbs 5:20)*

In the NLT it is translated “captivated.” Other translations use words like “enraptured” (NKJV), “exhilarated” (NAS) and “ravished” (KJV). All of these words carry the idea of being overwhelmed and even controlled. A captive is a person controlled by someone or something else. Someone who is intoxicated is someone controlled by a substance.

Sex is powerful and it can control us. Our sex drive can make us behave in ways that, good or bad, we might not ordinarily behave. It is a captivating, intoxicating power. In verse 19, the word “intoxicated” is used in a positive sense. Solomon admonishes you to be intoxicated with love, but then in verse 20, he uses it as part of a warning. He admonishes you to not be intoxicated by lust. You see, your sex drive can either lead you to love or to lust. Either place can overwhelm and control you. One place will bless you and the other will cause immeasurable harm.

These are the two overarching lessons Solomon has for us when it comes to sex. Embrace love and avoid lust. Let love control you, not lust. This can be one of life’s greatest battles and one of your most consequential choices. You can be captivated by love or by lust. Either way, you are controlled. One leads to life and the other to death.

Let Love Captivate You

The purpose of sex is to lead you to love, the kind of love your heart craves the most. God made your physical body and he made you to respond sexually. Sex is not a bad thing because it is a God-thing. God made sex and God made you.

As a part of that design, He included something wonderful for your sexual fulfillment. He has even designed you biologically to be captivated or addicted to a sexual relationship with one person. The key is to be captivated by the right thing. Proverbs 5 makes it very clear as to the kind of relationship in which you are invited to enjoy sexual love. What did Solomon say? Drink water from your well. Share your love only with your wife. Be captivated by the wife of your youth.

As has been clear throughout the book of Proverbs, Solomon directed this book to the next generation, from the perspective of one male talking to another. In chapter 5, he clearly begins by talking to "my son" only to broaden his address in verse 7 and make it plural, "my sons." He is writing to the next generation of men and he advises them to find their sexual fulfillment in the "wife of your youth." (5:18)

God has designed for sexual intimacy to be found in a relationship between a man and a woman who choose to come together, commit themselves to one another and live a life of exclusive love and commitment. It is within that context alone that God invites two people to discover His great blessing of intimacy through sexual fulfillment. This design by God is clear in the Bible. While the Bible *describes* many kinds of relationships, it *prescribes* only one kind of sexual relationship. In the very beginning, God created male and female. At that moment, He made us sexual, in order that…

> *…a man leaves his father and mother and is united to his wife, and they become one flesh.*
> *(Genesis 2:24)*

God has designed you for intimacy, but His plan requires that you follow certain steps in order for you to be capable of experiencing the depth of intimacy He has intended. God's plan for every person is first to *grow up (a man leaves his father and mother).* A person grows up and becomes independent of their parents. They learn a trade, get a job and provide for themselves. Then they may *step up (and is united to his wife).* A person makes a loyal, exclusive commitment to another person. We call this commitment marriage. It means to stick to another person. It is then that they can *go up,* as in go up into the bedroom (*they become one flesh).* Grow up, step up, and then go up. When you get it in that order, you are best prepared to enjoy God blessing of intimacy. When you don't grow up, and then step up, before you go up, you're bound to mess up.

Intimacy is a blessing that God longs to see you experience. It is something that we were created to desire even more than sex. Intimacy is often explained as, "into me you see." It is a state of being fully known and fully loved. It is when someone truly knows you for who you are, warts and all, and loves you unconditionally. We all want and need that kind of love and it is for this kind of love that God placed a strong sexual drive within you so that in the right place and at the right time you would be drawn to someone who can love you fully and whom you could love back.

Just like someone can be addicted to the wrong things, they can also be addicted to or captivated by the right things. God has hard wired our bodies to be captivated by one person. It is within that exclusive and honest relationship that we can find that which our hearts crave: real love and real intimacy. When we keep sex in its proper boundary, it can be used for its greatest good and produces the rich blessing God intended.

But there is an enemy to this kind of love. The great enemy of intimacy is promiscuity. Promiscuity is when you share yourself sexually with someone other than the person God has prepared for you. It is sexual activity beyond the bounds of that person with whom you have made an exclusive, loyal and loving commitment in marriage. Notice again what Proverbs 5:15-16 said,

Should your springs overflow in the streets, your streams of water in the public squares? Let them be yours alone, never to be shared with strangers.
(Proverbs 5:15-16)

The problem with promiscuity is not that it makes too much of sex, but that it doesn't make enough of sex. It isn't that you're getting too much, you're actually getting too little. The choice to share yourself sexually with someone other than a loving, committed husband or wife is to compromise yourself and settle for something that is far less than God's best. It is the choice to enjoy pleasure today and sacrifice the greater pleasure tomorrow. It is a failure to trust God's plan and a failure to trust Him with your future. The choice of promiscuity today can eradicate the blessing of God for tomorrow.

There is something beautiful, thrilling and exciting about sharing yourself with one person, knowing that person intimately and being known intimately, loving and being loved. This is what God has for you. He created you a sexual person so that you could one day be captivated by real love. It's why people can fall in love today and stay in love for a lifetime. It doesn't happen as much as it should, likely because many of us have messed the relational thing up, but it does still happen. People fall in love and stay in love for 40, 50 and 60 years or more, and they aren't tired and bored. You'll find couples that have been together decades that still cherish and honor one another. Why? Because they are captivated.

If you want the love of a lifetime, you won't find it on the road of promiscuity. You find it by making a commitment to purity and being faithful to the one you love or will love.

Purity is the pathway to intimacy. Promiscuity is not going to take you where you want to go. Do you really think that you can hang out at singles bars, have sex with all kinds of people and then one day have a relationship where you can be truly intimate with another person, spend your lives together and know the greatest happiness God intends for you to know? Do you think the path to promiscuity is going to get you there? No. Purity is the pathway to intimacy.

What if you are single? What if you have not found that person yet? Should you still stay pure? Is God really asking you to avoid sexual gratification with another person until marriage? Yes, absolutely yes.

Most singles hope to get married someday and most will. You may be in that group and your future relationship will be determined by your choices today. I can guarantee it. Even though you cannot see tomorrow, God sees tomorrow like you see this morning. The choice to remain pure is the choice to sacrifice something today in order to get something bigger tomorrow. That doesn't sound like sacrifice. It sounds more like an investment, an investment in your future. Placing a boundary is when you limit your freedom today so that you can increase your freedom tomorrow. Today's "no" opens the door to tomorrow's "yes," but today's compromise can forfeit tomorrow's blessing. When you choose to live a promiscuous life today, you are sacrificing tomorrow's treasure for something that is gone in a moment.

Some of you may live your entire life single, or at least a great portion of it. The Bible says that is a perfectly acceptable way to live and, in fact, there are even advantages. The single life has both advantages and disadvantages, while being single does not justify promiscuity. Promiscuity still doesn't take you where you want to go. If you are single, you need to learn to live grateful for God's gracious provisions in your life today. Nobody has every blessing all the time. No one. There may be some blessings that you will not enjoy and sexual intimacy may be one of those. Yet, there are other blessings that God has chosen only for you and choosing purity is still a key step to enjoying those blessings. Besides, you never know what God has planned for your future. Choose to trust Him today and He will remain just as trustworthy tomorrow.

Chose purity and you will be on the path to experience the deepest level of relationships that God has designed. But Solomon's words also come with a stern and sobering warning. Just as love can captivate you, so can immorality. Thus the second part of Solomon's advice is to avoid the captivity of immorality.

Avoid the Captivity of Immorality

In verse 20, Solomon warned, *"Don't be captivated, my son, by an immoral woman."* Don't be captivated by lust and sexual sin. Sexual sin can hold you captive like few things in this world. Just as sex can be used to "addict" us to one person, creating a lifelong love affair, sex can also stick us to other things. Few things are as hard to break today as sexual addictions. Addictions to pornography, same-sex attractions, various fetishes and behaviors can be powerful attractions that hold us in bondage and keep us from God's will and His gift of intimacy. Many psychiatrists claim that addictions to pornography can be as powerful, or even more powerful, than addictions to cocaine and heroin.[20] Given over to pornography, our brains become chemically programmed to crave and desire certain fulfillments that will carry us far away from God's plan and distort His beautiful gift.

I have been a pastor for more than 30 years and there is nothing I've seen that has caused more pain and heartbreak than sexual sin and bondage. I've seen grown men reduced to tears as they realize the consequences of their choices. I've watched people in a daze try to process how their world came crashing down. I've seen families destroyed, ministries lost, reputations trashed along with public shame, ridicule and the deep heartbreak of bringing pain to someone you love.

If you think you are immune to this, you must think you are more spiritual than David, stronger than Samson and wiser than Solomon. This is a lifelong battle. I read a story where the Buddha was explaining to his closest disciples how to live a celibate life. Celibacy is a requirement for Buddhist monks and so he was instructing them on how to avoid temptation. One of his followers asked, "How should a monk behave toward women?" The Buddha replied, "Avoid the sight of them." The disciple persisted, "But suppose we do see a woman?" The Buddha added, "Do not speak to her." The disciple persisted again, "But suppose she speaks to us," and then the Buddha said, "Then you must watch out."[21]

I think we need better advice than "watch out" and thankfully, Solomon has it for us. His counsel can be condensed into three points of advice for winning the war against immorality in your life.

First, *recognize the trap.* Sexual sin is a trap. A trap is a lie, a deception cleverly disguised to trick someone or something. A fisherman baits the hook. He disguises it. The fish sees the bait and thinks he is getting a free meal. She bites down only to realize it was a trick. She's trapped and will likely pay with her life. The mouse sees a free piece of cheese and then he wanders into a trap as the hammer swings down and smashes his head. A sleazy salesman tricks an unsuspecting consumer into making a foolish purchase. He doesn't tell the truth about the product and hides important details in the fine print. The naïve consumer signs the deal and is now trapped into a contract that he would never have agreed to if he had all the facts.

Sexual sin is like that. It is a trap laid by your spiritual enemy. He uses lies and deception to draw you in at your weakness until it is too late to escape. In Proverbs 7 Solomon describes a young man walking right into a trap. He wrote:

While I was at the window of my house, looking through the curtain, I saw some naive young men, and one in particular who lacked common sense.
(Proverbs 7:6-7)

Common sense is wisdom and this guy doesn't have any. Solomon continues,

He was crossing the street near the house of an immoral woman, strolling down the path by her house. It was at twilight, in the evening, as deep darkness fell.
(Proverbs 7:8-9)

Do you see the picture? It's getting dark and here is our guy walking down the street in the neighborhood of an immoral woman. He knows she's immoral. This guy crosses the street over to her side. He walks by her house and slows down. He knows where he is and he knows what he's looking for.

The woman approached him, seductively dressed and sly of heart. She was the brash, rebellious type, never content to stay at home. She is often in the streets and markets, soliciting at every corner. She threw her arms around him and kissed him, and with a brazen look she said, "I've just made my peace offerings and fulfilled my vows. You're the one I was looking for! I came out to find you, and here you are.
(Proverbs 7:10-15)

This isn't a shock. He was in the wrong place at the wrong time and a seductive woman greeted him with flattery.

> *My bed is spread with beautiful blankets, with colored sheets of Egyptian linen. I've perfumed my bed with myrrh, aloes, and cinnamon. Come, let's drink our fill of love until morning. Let's enjoy each other's caresses,*
> *(Proverbs 7:16-17)*

She offers to have sex with him. The very thing he has been fantasizing about and flirting with is his for the taking. Not only that, but she promises they won't get caught.

> *...for my husband is not home. He's away on a long trip. He has taken a wallet full of money with him and won't return until later this month.*
> *(Proverbs 7:19-20)*

She allures him with her seductive appearance, flattering speech and promise of easy sex with no consequences. But all of this is a lie, a deceptive trap. He will get caught and the consequences will be severe.

> *All at once he followed her like an ox going to the slaughter, like a deer stepping into a noose till an arrow pierces his liver, like a bird darting into a snare, little knowing it will cost him his life. Now then, my sons, listen to me; pay attention to what I say. Do not let your heart turn to her ways or stray into her paths. Many are the victims she has brought down; her slain are a mighty throng. Her house is a highway to the grave, leading down to the chambers of death.*
> *(Proverbs 7:22-27)*

The promise of sexual pleasure outside of God's design is a cruel lie that targets our vulnerability. Sometimes that vulnerability is sexual desire. Sometimes it is emotional loneliness or insecurity. It might even be a desire for real love and yet we are tricked into believing that sex will take us down a road that leads us to real love and intimacy. But it is a lie. It is a trap. Sexual sin takes us away from what we really want and need and leads us down a path of isolation, shame and loneliness. If purity is the pathway to intimacy, promiscuity is the pathway to isolation.

One of the biggest lies being sold today is the lie that *it's just sex.* In popular culture, the lie is this: *Sex is just physical.* For many, sex is little more than recreation or a meaningless physical act. Sort of like if you're hungry, you eat, if you're thirsty, you drink, and if you're motivated to have sex, you just have sex. No big deal…it's just physical.

We live in a day where it's a bigger deal to lose your iPhone than it is to lose your virginity. Just as it is a lie to think that sex is only physical, it is also a lie to believe that the physical act of intercourse does not affect your heart and your soul. Sex is not just physical. It is emotional and spiritual. That is why when children are violated they can struggle with the emotional and psychological scars all their lives. It is why rape is so devastating. If somebody sits down with me and says, "I've got to tell you something I've never told anyone, something I've been carrying around for a long time," I usually know what the person is going to say. Most of the time, it's going to be about sex—what they did, what somebody did to them, what they did as a result of what somebody did to them—but it almost always comes back to that, because sex is not just physical and deep down you already know that.

Those are just a few of the lies that weave the trap. Some other huge lies that the enemy wants you to buy are that you won't get caught and that there will be no consequences. But there are consequences—huge consequences. There are life altering and even eternity shaping consequences. Remembering those is the second important piece of advice to win the war against immorality.

Remember the Consequences. To avoid sexual immorality you need to take some time and think about where the road leads. I once heard of a man in the country who ignored a "road-closed" sign on a desolate stretch of highway. The sign warned that a bridge was out ahead, but the man felt sure that the sign was in error. So he traveled several miles and felt a tinge of smugness as he drove over a bridge that was obviously intact, but just a few miles later the man came upon a second bridge and, sure enough, the bridge was out. Angrily, he turned around and backtracked for miles until he could see in the distance the very sign whose warning he had ignored. As he got closer, he noticed that someone had written on the back of the sign with a black marker. The words read: "Welcome Back Stupid." We've all ignored some signs in our lives only to learn that we are not the exception.

You don't have to experience the pain of sexual sin. The warning signs and the consequences are there for all to see. You will not be the exception. Another warning of the fallout of sexual sin is in Proverbs 5:9-14,

> *...lest you lose your honor to others and your dignity to one who is cruel, lest strangers feast on your wealth and your toil enrich the house of another. At the end of your life you will groan, when your flesh and body are spent. You will say, "How I hated discipline! How my heart spurned correction! I would*

not obey my teachers or turn my ear to my instructors. And I was soon in serious trouble in the assembly of God's people."
(Proverbs 5:9-14)

Look at everything that Solomon warns can go wrong! You will lose your honor and dignity. You will experience cruelty. People you don't even know will end up with your possessions and money (ask anyone who has ever been through a divorce about that one.) You will groan in physical pain (ask anyone who has a venereal disease or who has had a loved one die of AIDS.) Your fellowship with God's people will be broken. The pain of sexual sin is physical, emotional, relational, financial and spiritual. It just isn't worth it.

The third piece of advice for avoiding the captivity of immorality is to r*etreat from temptation.* How do you respond to temptation? You run. Solomon advised,

Now then, my sons, listen to me; do not turn aside from what I say. Keep to a path far from her, do not go near the door of her house.
(Proverbs 5:7-8)

Retreat from temptation. Keep to a path far away. Don't even go near it. In chapter seven, the person Solomon describes as falling into the trap of immorality was flirting with disaster. He walked by the immoral woman's home at twilight. He loitered around a pit of debauchery and it is no surprise that he fell right in.

When it comes to sexual temptation don't fight, don't flirt, don't fold, just flee. Sexual immorality is something you must evade at all costs. You can't flirt with it and you can't fight with it. If you do, you're bound to fall. When you toy with temptation, be it through text, Facebook, or face-to-face conversations, you are willingly playing with fire. You're not strong enough or spiritual enough to flirt with this. No one is. Don't hang around people with low morals and don't go places where you know temptation lies. Some of the smartest, strongest and, yes, even most spiritual people have fallen into this trap. It's happened to pastors and politicians, businesspeople and talented athletes. It's happened to the determined and the disciplined, the incredibly smart and most respected. It can happen to you. Solomon says you better stay away from temptation. Flee from it.

In order to flee sexual temptation, you must pay attention to the signs and the lines. The signs are the direction you are headed and the lines are the boundaries you embrace.

Pay attention to the signs. Are you headed toward sexual sin or away from it? When students ask, "How close can I get to the edge without falling off," I already know they are too close. Why? They are headed in the wrong direction. When sexual sin becomes a public scandal, it's usually the last step or the consequence that we're seeing. We all see the public disgrace, the unplanned pregnancy, or the newsworthy scandal, but it never comes from one bad step. Sexual sin and the resulting fallout always come from a series of bad choices. Are you headed toward the edge or away from it? To flee sexual immorality is to go in a different direction and pursue the glory and purpose of God for your life. Don't go near the edge. Run in the opposite direction.

Pay attention to the lines. Everyone needs boundaries. I once heard of a wealthy woman who wanted to hire a new chauffeur. To help her decide who to hire she created a test. The test was to show the would-be chauffeurs a windy, mountain road and then ask how close they could get to the edge without falling off. The first candidate replied that he was such a skilled driver that he could get right up to the edge but never fall off. The second, trying to outdo the first, boasted that he could actually hang two tires over the edge and still maintain control of the car and not fall off. The third succinctly replied, "I wouldn't get anywhere near the edge." He got the job. The key is to stay away from the edge and the best way to do that is to have some boundaries and guardrails firmly positioned in your life.

Here's a little acrostic I've developed for some L-I-N-E-S that you can draw in your life.

L- LOOK:

Be careful how you look. Dress modestly. You can be stylish and attractive without overtly accentuating your sexuality. In fact the Bible commands it.

> *...adorn themselves in respectable apparel, with modesty and self-control,*
> *(1 Timothy 2:9)*

I- INTERNET PORN:

This is the plague of our culture. Porn is a perfect storm because it is anonymous, accessible and addictive. It is a trap, just as addictive as drugs, that draws a person in and holds them captive. Many people today are battling lifelong addictions to pornography that started with what they thought was a private, simple act. Now they are hooked. Porn distorts the truth about the opposite sex, especially women, and it distorts the act of sex itself. Porn is fantasy, not reality, and it is degenerative. It brings the viewer further and further into a dark web of corruption and can begin to facilitate attractions to any number of deviant and harmful sexual practices. Many convicted rapists talk about developing an addiction to porn that connected sex with violence. The infamous serial killer Ted Bundy spoke of how his addiction to porn took him deeper and deeper into depravity and eventually violence.[22]

Now, porn may not lead every person to the same place, or at the same rate, but there is an addictive effect that can create a greater and greater thirst for more perverse and explicit material. It can take you where you don't want to go.

There are many filters and accountability devices that can help you fight an addiction to porn. If you need help, ask for it and don't let this addiction ruin your life. People who struggle with this battle usually find they need to confess their struggle to someone and have some measure of accountability to help them stay in control. Draw some lines and don't drive outside the boundaries.

N - NO COMPROMISING SITUATIONS:

The Bible says to,

Abstain from all appearance of evil.

(I Thessalonians 5:22)

Be careful about putting yourself in places and situations where you are likely to be tempted to fall. Avoid the kinds of relationships that target your weakness. Guard your dating life. Be careful about being alone. The devil targeted Jesus when he was hungry, alone and tired. Be wise enough not to put yourself in situations where you are prone to fail.

E – ENTERTAINMENT:

The entertainment industry has probably done more to attack biblical sexual values than any other single area. Movies, music and television have all become a stage to flaunt sexual immorality as if it were the road to freedom. Be careful what you put into your mind. Little by little the wrong types of entertainment desensitize you to God's standards of right and wrong and set you up for believing the lies about sex. We all love entertainment, but be careful that you keep boundaries in place so that your entertainment choices don't become a doorway to an entanglement with false values.

S - SOCIAL MEDIA:

This is the age of social media. Facebook, twitter, and other new avenues of social connection are coming out daily. Like any medium, social media can be used for good. It connects us with friends and is even used to spread the gospel, but social media can also become an occasion for evil. More studies are linking Facebook contacts to divorce, affairs and immoral relationships. Many students have wandered into destructive and even dangerous relationships because they were not careful with their online activity. What happens in secret will usually become public at some point. Don't write things you will later regret or post pictures that will destroy your reputation. Make sure you have boundaries in place so that your use of social media doesn't become a stumbling block that takes you down.

Remember, sex is a good gift created by a good God to draw you into the intimacy that your heart truly craves. Sadly, the lies about sex are all around us and it is becoming more and more rare to see a person embrace biblical purity as their own personal standard. Culture may change, but the truth never does. God's design and plan are still as true and right as they ever were. Purity still leads to intimacy. Promiscuity stills leads to isolation. Embracing biblical purity may not be easy and it may not be popular, but it is still the right thing to do and the right path to take to find the best future God has for you.

Letter Seven
Work:
Blood, Sweat & Tears

Dear Son,

God has something for you to do. From the very beginning, when God made the first man, He designed him to do things. Adam was to work with God to manage the rest of God's creation. You were made to work. Work is a wonderful thing. It brings fulfillment, meaning and the joy of accomplishment. It's what we do. So, let's get to it.

They create, manage, lead, defend, enforce, inspire, equip, fix, construct, instruct, heal, administer and on and on. We do stuff. At least we're supposed to.

Unfortunately, in modern culture we've created a new class of permanent adolescence. For most of history, boys grew into men, left their homes, prepared for a vocation, took a job (a real job), married a woman, had children with her, protected and provided for his family and made his dent in the world. A man does not sit on his parent's couch playing video games, waiting for his mom to bring him mac-n-cheese. That's OK when you are a boy, but it's time to become a man. It's time to prepare and then seize the day. It's time to get to work.

Never live as if someone owes you anything. The United States government does not owe you anything. The city, the state, the Church, your parents, or your grandparents don't owe you anything. Life will not be brought to you on some silver platter. Don't march around carrying signs expressing your anger that society hasn't done something for you, or that some rich person hasn't given you enough, or that you're mad because someone has something you don't have. Here's the deal. I don't care if you're part of the 1% or the 99% or anything in between. You are part of the 100% who better figure out that life isn't fair and the world doesn't owe you a living. You had better get up, find a job and do something for somebody. That's how the world works. You provide something of value to someone else and they give you money for it.

Be grateful you live in this country. Be grateful for those who have given and defended your freedom. Be grateful to your parents and grandparents. Your grandfather, my father, was the 9th of nine children in a mill village in South Carolina. He grew up in a 2-bedroom house, served his country, put himself through night school and, except for about 2 weeks a year, got up Monday through Friday and went to work. He gave me opportunities he didn't have and I've been able to pass some along to you. Make the most of them. No one owes you anything. You owe them, so get busy.

Work is hard. That's why they call it work. But there is honor and fulfillment in a job well done. Whatever you decide to do, give it your best. Work hard. Make a difference. There will be time to rest and play. That, too, is part of life, but it only has real value when you've worked hard. Go the second mile. The road is never over crowded on the 2nd mile. Never meet expectations–exceed them! Show up on time. Be honest. If a person hires you, be the guy they can trust with their checkbook, their family, their business and their good name.

I can't promise you riches or fame, but I can promise you hard work leads to profit and personal fulfillment. You have opportunities most people in this world can only dream of. Don't flitter away precious time with laziness, games and silliness. Give it your best and then give it a little more.

The next four years are time to prepare, but prepare with a purpose. Prepare like you're going to work for the rest of your life because you probably will. Nothing great was ever accomplished without hard work. So the sun is up, the day is ahead, let's get to work!

Love,

Dad

Chapter Seven

Work: Blood, Sweat & Tears

All hard work brings a profit, but mere talk leads only to poverty.
(Proverbs 14:23)

Many people consider "work" a four-letter word in more ways than one. They spend numerous hours at work planning the days when they don't have to work. If you're like most people, you often daydream about the next vacation that will take you away from whatever fills the better part of your days. Maybe you wake up to your alarm each morning motivated only by the dream of a time when you won't have to work at all anymore. For so many people, work is burdensome and unrewarding. Oftentimes people's vocational situations are extraordinarily difficult and their job environments are anything but ideal. In many circumstances, people labor in conditions or surroundings that suck the life and purpose out of them. Others live with the frustration of not being able to find the "right" job. Even more find themselves between jobs and doing everything they can to find some kind of work at all. Countless graduates today walk into a marketplace having invested time, energy and a small fortune only to find limited opportunities and bad options. It's no wonder people think of "work" as a curse word, but the truth is, it's not. We live in a generation that desperately needs to recover a sense of what real work is all about and why it's so fundamentally important, even essential, to a life of fulfillment and purpose.

Adolescence is a 20th century invention. It wasn't something that previous generations had, or could much less afford. In most generations, when a boy's voice got deep and his body sprouted some hair, he figured out real quick that he'd better do something with his life. So, he chose a vocation, made some preparations, left his parents, went to work, found a woman to marry, had some kids and took care of his family. But then we invented this thing called adolescence. At first it spanned about six months, then someone extended it to a year, then to three years, and now some say it's a stage that starts around age twelve and continues to about thirty.

One of the most popular proposals in the health insurance reforms undertaken by President Obama's administration allows children to stay on their parent's health insurance policy until they are twenty-five. Not to be outdone, a Republican congressman proposed allowing children up to the age of thirty to be carried by their parent's health insurance provider. Now my intention is not to wade into that debate, but I have to admit that I thought, "Thirty? Really?" Should the world's children and the age of thirty be equated? Should a thirty-year old man or woman be called a dependent? David was thirty when he became King of Israel. When Joseph was thirty, he was one of the most powerful men on the planet. Jesus was thirty when he began His public ministry. Should "adolescence" now extend to thirty?

As one of the wealthiest men who ever lived, Solomon never needed to work a day in his life. He also could have insured that his children would never work a single day in their lives, but he never considered it. Solomon had a great deal to say about the value of hard work and the danger of laziness. This was a truth that he was intent to imbed in the next generation.

All hard work brings a profit, but mere talk leads only to poverty.
(Proverbs 14:23)

Like many of Solomon's principles, he presents a contrast between people who merely talk a good game from the sidelines and those who really do work hard. You know the people who are always chattering about what they would do in a given situation, or what they will do, or could do. You know the difference between those who just talk and those who step up and actually do something. Solomon draws out not only the difference but also a fundamental principle: all hard work leads to profit.

So what does that mean? Does it mean that if you work hard, you are sure to get rich? Of course not. The principle goes much deeper than that. In life, there will always be people who have more than others. It may seem unfair to you, but it's just the way it is and always will be. If everybody is rich, then nobody is really rich, right? Societies that have tried to make everything equal have only succeeded in making everyone poor. In those systems the people in power are usually the only ones who do become wealthy and often they are extremely corrupt. The name for that type of economic system is communism and it was one of the 20th century's spectacular failures. It just doesn't work.

There are a number of factors that will determine how much money you will earn in your life. Your context, your talent, your work ethic and your vocational choice are just a few. With a little bit of research and the answers to three specific questions, you can roughly determine what your financial status might look like. The questions you must ask are: What do you do? Where do you do it? How well do you do it? Your answers to these questions will govern how much you are able to accumulate in your life, but remember, the amount of money you acquire in a lifetime doesn't determine the significance of your life. Your self-worth is not subject to your net worth. What I'm talking about isn't a formula for getting rich; it is a formula for having a rich life.

Hard work brings *profit.* There are two parts of that statement that we must focus on. First, look at the word profit. Profit means value. Hard work creates value and significance in life. It is impossible to have a meaningful life without it. Secondly, focus on the words *hard work.* Work requires great effort. It isn't easy and it isn't supposed to be. If you want to have a great life, you must understand that work itself has great meaning and that it requires great effort.

Work has Great Meaning

There is a great value in working hard. I'm not talking about financial value, although there can indeed be great financial value in hard work, but the message of Solomon is much bigger than that. There is an intrinsic, inherent, theological and spiritual value in working hard. God made us to work because that's the way God is.

You can't get past the first verse in Genesis without seeing it. In the beginning, God did something, right? He built something. He made something. He constructed something. In the beginning, God rested? Is that what it said? In the beginning, God took a day off? No. In the beginning, God created because that's who He is. He did something of value. Then the Bible said that He made man in His image. He made us like Him which means He made us to do something, to teach, to instruct, to enforce, to defend. God made us to do creative and meaningful things.

Unfortunately, out in the world lies a warped theology that claims work is a curse and completely misunderstands God's intent for it. This theology usually goes something like this,

> *In the beginning, God made Adam and Eve. He put them in a beautiful garden where they sat around all day eating grapes off of trees, fanning themselves with large leaves, and watching the clouds pass by. Then one day they messed up bad, real bad. So God said, "Because you messed up bad, and because the world has been corrupted, you are going to have to go to work." So He kicked them out of Club Med and told them to pull up their sleeves and get working and there you have it, the curse of God on the earth. (Thanks a lot, Adam and Eve.) But the good news is that one-day when we die, we'll get to go heaven and not have to work anymore. We'll all get to kick back on clouds, relax, and listen to Gabriel play the harp.*

I've actually heard sermons that sounded a lot like that, but if you go back and read the book of Genesis, here's what you'll really find. Before Adam and Eve ever sinned, before the world was ever tainted or corrupted, when God made man in His very own image, He gave him a job to do. He said,

> *"I want you to have dominion over the fish of the sea and the birds of the air. I want you to fill the earth and subdue it."*
> *(Genesis 1:28)*

Talk about a job description. Here is one guy and God says to him, "I want you to fill up the earth, and I want you to manage it, subdue it and have dominion over it." God gave Adam a job to do. God said, "Do something." He knew that when you do something of value, you will find enormous value. When you do something of meaning, you are operating like God Himself, the Great Architect of life. There is meaning in everything He does. God made us to do something important and without a meaningful job to do, life loses meaning altogether.

The Bible teaches us that work is God's gift to us, not His curse on us. Work is a gracious bounty bestowed upon you by God to help you become like Him and to add meaning and value to your life. I'm not talking about the value of your paycheck, or the value of your title; I'm talking about the value of what you choose to do with your life. There are plenty of moms who have chosen the great task of managing their homes and families and dedicating themselves to doing it well. That's important work with invaluable dividends that you won't see in a paycheck. I know people who have retired from earning a paycheck to pursue something else of great value that impacts more people than they ever could have in their paying job. What is it you're doing every day? What are you managing? What are you building? Who are you leading? What are you creating? What difference are you making? Your ability and even your need to work are benefits from a gracious God.

Theodore Roosevelt said, "Extend pity to no man because he has to work. If he is worth his salt, he will work. I envy the man who has work worth doing and does it well. There never has been devised, and there never will be devised, any law which will enable a man to succeed save by the exercise of those qualities which have always been the prerequisites of success, the qualities of hard work, of keen intelligence, of unflinching will."[23]

When you take the element of work out of someone's life, you may think you're helping him or her, but you're not. You're disempowering them. You're undercutting them. We do a great disservice to people when we think that we're helping them by giving something to them and yet don't help them work.

Robert Lupton wrote a book entitled *Toxic Charity.* Although parts of his book have been somewhat controversial and you may disagree with his view on some matters, his four decades of working with the poor and the homeless in Atlanta, Georgia give credence to his thesis. He states that much of what people do in order to try to help others only makes the problem worse. Lupton wrote, "When we do for those in need what they have the capacity to do for themselves, we disempower them."[24] If we take from the rich to give to the poor in the name of fairness without embracing the value of meaningful work, we aren't playing Robin Hood, we're defying the will of our Maker.

Certainly we should give generously. Solomon specifically wrote about the importance of generosity and the Bible teaches throughout that we should joyfully give to others without expecting anything in return, but if we confuse generous giving with the kind of toxic charity that enables people to live without work, we are robbing them of something more valuable than money. We are robbing them of real significance in life. I'm not talking about those who would gladly work but can't. I'm not talking about people who, because of frailty in life, or because of disease or handicap are unable to work. We're talking about those who can work but don't.

The same apostle Paul who collected offerings from the church to give to the poor and encouraged all people to live generous lives wrote these words:

"If a man will not work, he shall not eat."
(2 Thessalonians 3:10)

That may sound callous, but Paul was dealing with the same stuff that we deal with today. While he encouraged everyone to be generous, he also understood that there are some people who are content to be free loaders in the church. So he laid down a rule. He said that if a person doesn't want to work, tell them they shouldn't eat.

> *If anyone does not provide for his relatives, and especially for his immediate family, he has denied the faith and is worse than an unbeliever.*
> *(1 Timothy 5:8)*

Once again, Paul was not being harsh when he made this statement. He is asserting that work is one of God's gifts to us and that as believers we must not waste it. Instead, what we do with our work becomes our tribute back to God. The Bible teaches that everything we do should be done as unto the Lord. The fact that God gave you the ability, the strength, the creativity and the mind to work is a gift from Him and brings value into your life. How you use those abilities will either honor the Giver or won't. What you do with your time says to Him, "This is what I think of You, Lord. This is how I value the blessings You have given me." So are you going to merely work for the praise of man or for just a paycheck? Or are you going to take the abilities that God has gifted you with and seek to uncover meaning and bring God glory? Are you going to mean it when you say to the Lord, "Everything I do, Lord, is for Your glory"?

I've thought a lot about the concept of work as I've poured through Solomon's wisdom on the topic and studied God's commands throughout the Bible, and as I look around I've come to the conclusion that when someone sits idle, choosing not to work when they can, it's not because they feel badly about themselves. Instead, it's a display of how they view God. It shows that a person thinks that God isn't worth his very best and that His glory doesn't deserve his greatest effort. It is a person's warped view of God that is messing him up, not his opinion of himself. A person's attitude about himself or herself will ultimately be determined by what he thinks about God. William Bennett wrote, "*Hard work is what I do with my living, not for my living.*"[25]

We need to revolutionize this idea of work. It's time we challenge our thinking and decide that it's not about what I do for my living, but it's about what I do with my life. It's the contribution I make that is worth something. Solomon didn't have to work a day in his life, but he understood the intrinsic value of doing something with his life.

Another myth that often slips into church life is that some work is spiritual, but most is not. This delusion promotes the dangerous idea that work that isn't within a vocational ministry setting has no spiritual value and does not contribute to the building of God's kingdom. Occasionally people will come to faith in Christ and in their newfound enthusiasm assume that if they are really serious about their faith they must quit their jobs to pursue vocational ministry. They believe that it's the spiritual thing to do and will bring them closer to God. Such a destructive idea sets people up for failure and disappointment and it undermines the value that God places on work.

Certainly there are some vocations that do not honor God or further His purpose. As Christians, we should avoid those that violate our convictions and bring harm to others or ourselves. But beyond those obvious examples, there is a vast universe of opportunity to earn a living, contribute to the needs of society and create a platform to honor and glorify God in the process. A great business can glorify God. A great teacher can influence lives. A great doctor can minister more than medicine. God can work in and through ordinary people in seemingly ordinary vocations to accomplish His purpose.

There will always be people that God gifts and calls to lead and teach His Church. I knew when I was 14 years old that it was God's purpose for my life. Some people will tell you that God called them into a special role of vocational ministry even later in their lives. If you are sensing that this may be God's purpose for you, let me encourage you to talk to other leaders and pray earnestly. If God is leading you in that direction, go for it with all your heart, but it is also important to know that you can serve God earnestly and with your whole heart in non-ministry vocations as well. Yes, we need pastors and church leaders, but we also need committed Christ followers in every area of society. Whatever you choose to do can be an act of worship to God and is part of your ministry whether it is "secular" (non-church related) or not.

If you have yet to make your career choice, look at every opportunity as a chance to serve God and live out His will for your life. If you are already in a job, realize that you don't have to quit doing what you do to have a ministry. Have a ministry right where you are. Make a difference in the lives of the people you're already working with. Understand that God has given you a platform to make an impact in the world right where you stand. Reform your thinking about work so that your focus is not on what you do for a living, but on what you can do with your life for the glory of God.

If God does stir your heart toward vocational ministry and service, by all means respond to that call, but whether you serve in a church or dig ditches beside a road, you must realize that work itself is one of the great gifts of life. Recovering that understanding will go a long way toward fulfilling God's purpose for your life and the result will be a life overflowing with meaning and joy.

So, the first thing you must learn is that work has great meaning. The second thing you must realize is that work requires great effort.

Work Requires Great Effort

Remember Solomon wrote in Proverbs 14:23 that *...**hard** work brings profit?* Well, he also had a lot to say about the dangers of laziness. In fact, he uses that word, sometimes translated sluggard, seventeen times. Here are some of the things Solomon said about laziness:

> *Lazy hands make a man poor,*
> *(Proverbs 10:4)*

> *Lazy people irritate their employers, like vinegar to the teeth or smoke in the eyes.*
> *(Proverbs 10:26)*

Have you ever gotten smoke in your eyes? It burns and irritates. If you hire a lazy person, that's what it is going to be like.

> *Work hard and become a leader; be lazy and become a slave.*
> *(Proverbs 12:24)*

> *A lazy person is as bad as someone who destroys things.*
> *(Proverbs 18:9)*

Can you imagine hiring a vandal and putting him on staff? Imagine hiring somebody and saying, "I'd like you to destroy things. I'd just like you to walk around, punch holes in the wall, tear things down and mess things up." Solomon says when you hire a person who is lazy and lacks a strong work ethic, it's like hiring someone to destroy things.

Solomon warns throughout Proverbs about the danger of lacking a proper work ethic. It's often that flawed view of work that contributes to a person's lack of motivation and their failure to put their heart into what they do. Because of this flawed view of work, the focus is placed on what it is they do *for* a living, not *with* their living.

As I read through each and every verse in Proverbs that discussed the importance of working hard, I observed several themes, several categories. I'm going to call them the "7-Up's" of hard work. Here are seven words of encouragement about how you can avoid laziness and understand the value of hard work:

Grow Up

Quit chasing fantasies and become an adult. It is time to go to work. You know what it's like when a person chases fantasies. A fantasy chaser is always telling you that they're *going* to do something. Something big is always going to happen to them. They're daydreamers. They're playing the lottery and waiting for some sure-fire, imaginary bonanza to come through. At some point you need to grow up. It's okay to wear blue tights and a cape and run around in the back yard pretending to be Batman when you're 8 years old, but when you're 25 and you're wasting all your time pretending to be Batman on the X-Box, that's not cool. It's time to grow up. It's time to quit chasing rainbows. Listen to Solomon:

A hard worker has plenty of food, but a person who chases fantasies has no sense.
(Proverbs 12:11)

He who works his land will have abundant food, but the one who chases fantasies will have his fill of poverty.
(Proverbs 28:19)

Lazy people take food in their hand but don't even lift it to their mouth.
(Proverbs 26:15)

People who are lazy won't carry out even the most basic tasks necessary for their lives and well-being. They can have food in their hand, but they want somebody else to lift it. That's what babies do. Little babies need Momma to feed them. The problem is, there are some young adults today still waiting for Momma to feed them.

Sure, growing up today has its challenges, but I'd like to say something to the parents, grandparents, aunts, uncles and whoever might be reading this book. If you are doing for others what they need to be doing for themselves, you are not only *not* helping them, but you are empowering them to live a self-destructive life. At some point, it's time to make them feed themselves. Quit doing it for them! Now some of you just took a deep breath. You're saying, "You don't understand. They're not doing it for themselves. They won't do it for themselves and I don't know what to do! How can I motivate them?" Do you really want to know? I recommend hunger. So did Solomon.

The laborer's appetite works for him; his hunger drives him on.
(Proverbs 16:26)

Hunger has a way of motivating a person. I know that sounds callous, but when you don't teach a person to work, you're not empowering them. They are not going to be what God wants them to be until they learn to lift their own spoon to their own mouth. Parents, you've got to let them grow up even if it's the hardest thing you'll ever watch.

Get Up

Get up! Don't sleep too much. Look, I've seen the surveys showing that Americans aren't sleeping enough. Sure, we all need a good night's sleep. That's fine, but Solomon describes plenty of lazy people today when he criticizes those who sleep too much. Some people just won't get up.

I understand that people have different work hours and their schedules dictate when they must sleep, but the key word there is "schedule." Some people are morning people. Some people's jobs require them to work at night. I get all of that, but if I'm talking to the majority of people who work during the daylight hours, I would say that I've never met too many successful people that rolled into work around 9:30 or 10:00 am. I just haven't. I mean, they may be there, but most of the people I've met who have accomplished or achieved something of significance were usually up early and knew how to tackle their day.

Proverbs 31 describes the hard-working woman as one who gets up before dawn and goes to work.

She gets up while it is still night; she provides food for her family...
(Proverbs 31:15)

But you, lazybones, how long will you sleep? When will you wake up?
(Proverbs 6:9)

Laziness brings on deep sleep; and the shiftless man goes hungry.
(Proverbs 19:15)

Do not love sleep or you will grow poor; stay awake and you will have food to spare.
(Proverbs 20:1)

As a door swings back and forth on its hinges, so the lazy person turns over in bed.
(Proverbs 26:14)

Isn't that a great proverb? A door goes back and forth on its hinges, but it doesn't go anywhere. It moves, but it doesn't do anything. Solomon says that it is the same way with someone who is lazy. They turn over and over on their bed, but they don't go anywhere. It's time to get up!

Shut Up

Quit making excuses. Have you ever noticed that people that are lazy and not industrious always have a reason why? They always have an excuse. There's always something that happened, always something that went wrong. There's always a reason why that job won't work, or that boss is rotten.

They've always got a reason. Solomon lost patience with that. He said,

> *The lazy person claims, "There's a lion out there! If I go outside, I might be killed!"*
> *(Proverbs 22:13)*

Lions were fairly common in the Middle East and you can read about a few of them in the Bible. In this verse, Solomon equates the fear of a lion with a lazy person that is always fearful of what could go wrong. When questions like, "Why don't you do this?" or "Why don't you start that?" start rolling in, a lazy person's reply is guarded by procrastination and coated in fear, "But there's a lion out there! I might get killed!"

> *The lazy person claims, "There's a lion on the road! Yes, I'm sure there's a lion out there!"*
> *(Proverbs 26:13)*

There will always be a reason not to do something. Benjamin Franklin wrote, "I never knew a man who was good at making excuses, who was good at anything else."[26] The reality is that there are lions out there, aren't there? There are people who are jerks. There are jobs that are hard. Somebody just might mistreat you. Things could go wrong. There are lions out there. Solomon wrote, *the lazy person is always worried about the lion.* Can I tell you what you've got to do when you grow up? You've got to walk out the door and slay the lion. That's what you've got to do.

I read about a shoe company that sent a salesman down to a small Caribbean island looking for a new market. After two days went by, the salesman called the company and said, "This is terrible. It won't work. I haven't sold any shoes. You need to bring me home. There is no market for our product here." Perplexed, his boss said, "Why not?" The discouraged salesman replied, "Nobody down here wears shoes." So the company brought him home. A few months later, they decided to try again and sent their best salesman to the same island. Three days passed and the salesman called the company in a panic, "You need to send more shoes! It's unbelievable. There's a huge market waiting for us down here!" Scratching his head, his boss said, "So what did you find?" The delighted salesman pronounced, "Nobody here has shoes and they all need them! It's a ground breaking opportunity!" You see, some people only see the obstacles in life and some people see the opportunities. Some people see problems and others see possibilities. While some people see the lions, there are others who say, "I'll figure out a way to get past the lion. I'm not going to let a few lions walking around keep me from making a difference."

Solomon wrote,

> *"If you wait for perfect conditions, you'll never get anything done."*
> *(Ecclesiastes 11:4, TLB)*

He was absolutely right. You've got to shut up and quit making excuses.

Wise Up

Listen to good advice. It's amazing how people that aren't being productive seem wise in their own eyes. Solomon, one of the wisest men who ever lived, was obsessed with getting counsel from other people. The wiser he got, the more wisdom he desired. The wiser he was, the more counselors he wanted. It's amazing to me how some people who are unproductive always think everyone else is dumb.

Lazy people consider themselves smarter than seven wise counselors.
(Proverbs 26:16)

We all need wise counsel. I sure don't have all the answers and neither do you. That is why wise and productive people are always listening to wiser and more productive people. They're always seeking careful insight and discerning wisdom. On the other hand, people who are lazy and unproductive seldom do.

Clean Up

You've got to be willing to do the dirty work. By dirty work, I don't mean unethical work; I mean the hard, nasty work that no one else wants to do. Some people think they're too good to do certain things. Can I let you in on a secret? No job is so glamorous that you don't have to do some dirty work. I love this verse in Proverbs.

Without oxen a stable stays clean, but you need a strong ox for a large harvest.
(Proverbs 14:4)

If you don't have anything in the stable, it's clean. There are no problems and no messes. It might look great, but that's all it offers because you're going to need a strong ox to have a large harvest. You're going to need to keep a big ox in the stable if you're planning on a big harvest, but there is a problem with a big ox. A big ox makes a big mess. Yep, piles everywhere. The bigger the ox the bigger the mess will be, and when the big ox makes a big mess, somebody's got to pick up a shovel and clean out the stable.

When you and I go to work, sometimes we have to pick up a shovel and clean up a mess. No job exists where you won't occasionally have to be willing to pick up your shovel, hold your nose and clean up a mess that the big ox made. An empty stable is clean, but you don't get any harvest. If you want a harvest, you've got to be willing to do the unpleasant jobs sometimes. If you want a big payoff, every once in a while you've got to pick up a shovel and do the stuff that's hard to do.

Show Up

Show up and do your job. Just showing up on time will get you ahead of most people. If you show up on time, all the time, then you'll separate yourself from the crowd. Make it a priority to arrive at work each day on time and do the job you've been asked to do well. Show up and keep showing up. I don't mean three days a week. I mean every day you're expected to be there. Now if you show up a little bit early and do a little bit more than is expected, you'll jump to the top 10% in the success category. Solomon wrote:

> *He who gathers crops in summer is a wise son, but he who sleeps during harvest is a disgraceful son.*
> *(Proverbs 10:5)*

He is saying that there is a proper time to show up.

> *Those too lazy to plow in the right season will have no food at the harvest.*
> *(Proverbs 20:4)*

Once you show up, do the job and do it well.

Go Up

Get better at what you do. Find what it is that God has skilled you to do and then improve at it. I love this verse:

Do you see a man skilled in his work? He will serve before kings;
(Proverbs 22:29)

The more skilled you become at what you do, the more opportunities you will have and the greater impact you will see. Look for ways to continue improving and learning. Learn from those who are better than you are, listen to those who are wiser than you are and constantly watch the winners. You can always get better. You should never stop learning and improving. When you quit learning, you're done leading and soon you'll stop winning. So keep learning and keep improving. Get better. Go up.

So we can summarize what Solomon says about work in those two statements: work has great meaning and work requires great effort. Our view of work should come from God. He made us to value and pursue meaningful work. Our work is not primarily about making money. God designed you and shaped you to do specific things. The process of doing them with all your heart becomes your gift back to the Giver. It's becomes how you find value in your efforts. When you do something well and you do it for God's glory, it changes how you see your work and becomes a conduit of gratitude that impacts all those whom God puts in your path.

So be done with laziness, excuses and a false view of work. Work comes from God. Work brings value and meaning. Work is what we do with our lives that makes a difference in the world around us. Work is good. So let's get to work and work hard.

Letter Eight

God: The Choice that Matters Most

Dear Son,

And so the day has arrived. By any measurement your graduation from High School is a momentous occasion. There will be other milestones and other days may eventually hold more significance, but this is a big one. As much as any single event in our culture, it marks the end of childhood. So now what is the end of the matter? What is left to say?

In 18 years we have tried to convey many lessons. Most were simple guidelines, observations about life, directives and suggestions. Looking back I cannot believe how fast it has gone. I guess I always knew this day would come. I just didn't think it would be today. And now here it is. We've reached a critical juncture. Soon your freedom will expand, your autonomy will increase and you will begin from this day on to walk more and more on your own and assume the choices for your life. Our love will never diminish, but our role will change. And it is as it should be. From the beginning, this is the day we have worked for. This is your day. This is your time.

But before you go, a final word. One last thought before you turn the corner: Remember God. If you forget everything else, don't forget that. Don't forget Him. The scoffers will ignore God as an irrelevant vestige of the past. They will discount faith as some ancient attempt to control and manipulate. You will find many who will use their lives, their freedom, their autonomy to pursue the pleasures of the flesh, the possessions of life and to climb the ladders of success and fame intoxicated by the applause and acclaim of others. You can choose to do that, but you will waste your life if you do. For down those roads, perhaps unseen to you, lie the wreckage of untold millions who have spent their lives for all that lies "under the sun" only to find it empty. As one wise man said, "like chasing the wind."

And here is what you must know. This is not some dress rehearsal. This is it, your one life to live. And all too soon, sooner than you think it will be gone like an afternoon breeze. You, too, will grow old. Your youth will be gone and there are no do-overs. And life, as a general rule, doesn't get easier; in many ways it gets harder. It certainly gets harder the farther away from God you roam.

So here is my best counsel: Remember God while you are young. Do not forget the things you have learned, seen and witnessed. Remember the wisdom of His commands. Remember the unconditional love found in His grace. Remember the truth found in His word. And as you set your course for life, trust Him. Trust Him with all your heart. Trust that He sees a future you cannot yet see. Trust that His gracious hand will guide and direct your steps. Trust that He supplies a strength and power that will carry you through life's toughest moments. Realize the limits of human wisdom and understanding. Let Him lead. Choose to follow. This is His promise: He will direct your paths.

I remember your first steps. For 18 years we have tried, as best human and fallible parents could, to watch over your steps. It's hard for us now to watch you turn this corner. It is wonderful and hard all at the same time. We held you and fed you and rocked you. We held your hand in those first tentative steps in the yard. Caught you in those first jumps into the water. We comforted you and assured you and cajoled you and encouraged you. We breathed your name to God in prayer more than a few times. We asked God to bless and He has. We did all that and more and now it is time to let go. And as we do with grateful hearts we give this one final word: Remember God. Follow His hand. Trust His heart. He will lead you on and He will lead you home.

Love,

Dad

Chapter Eight

God: The Choice that Matters Most

Trust in the Lord with all your heart and lean not on your own understanding; in all your ways acknowledge him, and he shall direct your paths.
(Proverbs 3:5-6)

The day is coming. The day you must say good-bye. The day a child steps forward into adulthood and the parent lets go. The day arrives before you know it. In truth, it is a period of transition. The last year of high school comes to a close, graduation parties commence and the summer after the senior year feels like it was crammed into two weeks. The bags are packed and the car is loaded. It is gradual in one sense, but there are dramatic moments, meaningful ceremonies and poignant steps that do mark the change. There is a very real sense in which a moment represents a letting go, a stepping back and the fulfillment of a promise. It's a good thing and it is an emotional thing all rolled into one.

I have a friend from my teenage years named Debbie. We're the same age and we left for college at the same time. I'll never forget the story she told me about when she and her friend, Gaye, left for college all those years ago. It was that classic sentimental moment in her driveway when the last bag was loaded into the car and she was about to drive away from her parents and into her college years. You know how it goes. Everyone is crying and hugging. Parents are tossing out last minute advice like eighteen years just wasn't enough. "Lock your doors," "Here's some extra money," and "Don't forget to call," were thrown out like desperate Hail Mary passes in a football game. Debbie recounted that when she and Gaye finally got in the car, wiped away their tears and drove off, they got about a block away, turned the corner, and, she said, it hit them. Their tears turned to cheers as they yelled, "Yessss! We're freeee! We can stay out all night and they'll never know! They can't do a thing about it!" The best part was years later when her parents told her what happened back at the house around the same time. They wiped their tears, looked at one another, and went, "Yessss! We're freeee!"

It may be a high school graduation, or starting college, or moving away for the first time, but there will come a moment when you pass a milestone and it is time to go. It is at those moments when parents think about what we would say if we had just one more chance to impart some wisdom, one more shot at offering some advice. What do you say "before you go?"

In a sense, that is what this book has been about: some final summary, some bits of wisdom before you go. Have you ever tried to walk out the door and your parents are still spouting off some kind of advice? It is usually an irritating piece of obvious counsel that you have heard a hundred times before. "Say out of trouble." "Be careful." "Don't drive too fast." "Remember to call."

But what do you think they would say if they really just had one more chance, one final word?

I think it's important that every parent thinks about that "one more thing" they would want to say, that one thing that would be more important than any other that their child take with them when they leave home, because if you know the "one more thing" that you would say, you can start saying it now. That way when the moment comes, you'll know you've said it loud, clear and often.

When it came time for my youngest child to leave home, like a lot of parents, I began to wonder, "Did I say the things that I needed to say? Amidst all the noise and clamor, chaos and distractions, lessons and appointments, did I get across the thing that really mattered most?"

If you want to know what the most important bit of wisdom is, I am not sure you could do better than a father did in the Old Testament. In the book of Proverbs, a father wrote down principles and guidelines for life, and he passed them on to the next generation. Forty-five times in the book of Proverbs he used the word "son," and twenty-three times it was part of a command. Proverbs is Solomon's attempt to write down his observations on life and to hand it to the next generation. In this book, we've examined those sage segments of advice in eight different categories.

We've looked at what he had to say about love, lust and everything in between. We explored what he had to say about money, communication and friendships. We learned what he said about hard work and considered the importance of good character.

But if there was one final thing he would say to you before you walked out the door, I am convinced it would be this:

> *My son, do not forget my teaching, but keep my commands in your heart, for they will prolong your life many years and bring you prosperity. Let love and faithfulness never leave you; bind them around your neck, write them on the tablet of your heart. Then you will win favor and a good name in the sight of God and man. Trust in the Lord with all your heart and*

lean not on your own understanding; in all your ways acknowledge him, and he shall direct your paths. Be not wise in your own eyes; fear the Lord and shun evil. *(Proverbs 3:1-7)*

I think there are two things every parent wants to be able to say and every kid needs to hear. One is about your past and the other is about your future. One is a look back and the other is a look ahead. My prayer for my own children, as it is for every young man or woman who is embarking upon the path of independence, is that you will have a firm foundation on which to build your life and a Heavenly Father that you can follow for the rest of your life. I want you to leave with a foundation to remember and a Father you can follow. When you look at these seven verses, isn't that what Solomon is saying?

Remember What You've Learned

Look carefully at verse one,

My son, do not forget my teaching, but keep my commands in your heart,
(Proverbs 3:1)

Don't forget. Don't just casually remember the wisdom you've been taught, plant those precepts in your heart. Solomon is saying, "I want you to remember everything I've taught you." He said it again and again in this book. For instance, in Proverbs 6:20, he said:

My son, keep your father's commands and do not forsake your mother's teaching.
(Proverbs 6:20)

Now I know that I've made an assumption here, one that certainly isn't true in every case. I'm going to assume for the moment that someone has tried to lay a spiritual, biblical foundation in your life. I'm making that assumption because you are reading this book. Someone has placed it in your hands. Maybe it was a graduation gift. If so, then someone in your life wants you to hear the same wisdom Solomon passed down long ago. Maybe you picked it up yourself or someone recommended it to you. Even that was not a coincidence. If my assumption is not accurate in your life, don't dismay. God has a reason and a plan for you reading this right now and while a foundation of biblical truth may not have been laid in your life, He has still given you this chance to hear and respond to His truth.

If you did have a family that tried to plant spiritual seeds in your life, chances are they didn't do it perfectly. No one has. Your parents are flawed just like I'm flawed. No matter how hard they may have tried, they're probably thinking right now, "I wish I had done this better," or "I wish I hadn't done that." Not even the best parents are perfect parents. In all likelihood, one day you will get to see how hard this job called parenting really is.

I am one of those who has been blessed by a strong heritage of biblical faith. I have often thought back on many stories from my childhood, but the memories that really stand out are those that helped weave the spiritual heritage I was given. My parents took us to church every Sunday and much of my free time was spent participating in activities with my church youth group, but there is one particular scene from my childhood that tends to leap forward in my memory. It is a scene from Vacation Bible School where I was standing with my hand over my heart and I, along with dozens of other youngsters, were making pledges and commitments to various things. I remember beginning each day at VBS with pledges. Somebody brought in the American flag and we pledged to it.

That wasn't unusual because we did that every morning at school. That one we all knew well. Then someone brought in the Christian flag and we said a pledge to it. I had never seen a Christian flag. I thought maybe it was invented just for VBS. But the pledge I remember most of all was the pledge we made to the Bible. Some kid would hold up a Bible and we would all stand and recite a pledge that went like this:

> *"I pledge allegiance to the Bible, God's Holy Word, and I will make it a lamp unto my feet and a light unto my path, and I will hide its Word in my heart that I may not sin against God."*

I can go back in my mind to that very moment, as a little boy, standing in front of a Bible thinking, "I pledge allegiance. It's a lamp to my feet. It's a light unto my path. And if I will hide its words in my heart, it will keep me from sinning against God. This is the light. This is the lamp." Somehow in those pledges and somewhere along the way, I learned what my parents, my grandparents and other people in my life were trying to convey to me. This Bible is true. It is a light to your feet and a lamp to your path.

As you journey through life, you're going to face tough choices. You may be thinking that the choices you have are new and that no generation has ever faced those choices before, but you would be dead wrong about that because the same choices you're going to face are the same choices and the same tests that have plagued mankind from the very beginning. The fashions will change, the music will change, but the choices will always be the same. You're going to be tested in the same areas that your parents were tested. The same answers to your questions about life and how to find your way lie in the same truth that was available to them and will still be available to your children. God's Word, the Bible, is true. Maybe for you, just like it was for me, somewhere along the way somebody tried to teach you that.

The Bible is true. There is a God who loves you and cares for you and His principles for living provide the foundation you need for a life of meaning, purpose and happiness.

The spiritual and biblical lessons that you've been taught are meant to form a foundation on which to build, not walls meant to contain. I don't want you to look at God's truths and the lessons your parents taught you that were based on God's truths as high walls meant to constrain you. It is not that we don't want you to learn anything else or question anything you've ever heard. The truth is, you have so much more to learn. The very best leaders want you to keep learning.

I hope that you will continue to grow smarter and wiser and that you will learn and see things that the previous generations could only have imagined. I hope you do things in the world that innovate, create and bring change because the greatest innovations and creations usually come from the rising generations, not the established ones. That's the neat thing about being young. You see the world differently. You don't wear the same blinders of generations past, but instead look at the world and go, "Hey! Why can't we do it this way?" You are the reason the world changes and good things happen. You will see the world in creative, new and different ways. The spiritual lessons you were given in childhood aren't walls to hem you in, it's actually the complete opposite. These spiritual lessons, taken and applied, will form a foundation on which you can build higher and higher. Walls can change, but once the foundation is laid, it's pretty much there. The truth of God is the foundation on which you can build and the stronger the foundation is, the bigger the building can be.

In Jesus' great Sermon on the Mount recorded in Matthew 5-7, Jesus finished by talking about truth and the foundation it can provide. He said that when it comes to choosing a foundation, you get two options. You can be foolish and build your house on the sand, or you can build on a rock. Here's the thing about sand. It makes for a great day at the beach, but it's a terrible foundation for life. Sand is always changing. If you take a walk along the shore, it will look different today than it did yesterday because the tide washes in and out. You might build a little castle today, but tomorrow it will be gone. The tide goes in and out, the wind blows and storms come. Everything changes. If you try to build your life on what's popular or what feels good at the moment, you can rest assured that you are building on a faulty foundation that will soon be washed away. Remember what Solomon said,

> *There is a way that seems right to a man, but in the end it leads to death.*
> *(Proverbs 16:25)*

The problem with sand is that it's always shifting. I know it's popular today for people to think that you can determine truth by an opinion poll or an election, but if you decide what is true based on these things, you'll be wrong. You see, truth is true because it aligns with the character of God. The Bible says,

> *The grass withers and the flower fades, but the word of God stands forever.*
> *(Isaiah 40:8)*

Whatever is fashionable, cool or hip today is going to be out of fashion, un-cool, and unhip a few years from now. The truth of the Living God was true 50 years ago. It was true 100 years ago and even 1000 years ago. The truth of God will still be true 1000 years from now. The Bible is truth. It is the light under your feet and the lamp for your path. This Word of God is the only sure foundation on which to build. Solomon said,

"Remember the foundation you've been given." He wanted us to remember because he knew we would be tempted to forget.

I can promise you this: you will be tested. You're going to face testing real soon.

You're going to be tested in God's moral law. As you leave home there will be plenty of people inviting you to do things that violate your conscience and the boundaries of moral behavior you have been given. You can rest assured that the crowd isn't going in the right direction. You will be tested to compromise your convictions and ignore God's moral standards.

You're also going to be tested in God's doctrinal truth. You're going to talk to people who have questions you can't readily answer. You'll meet professors who are the smartest people you've ever been around and some of them will deliberately attack and undermine the Christian faith. Count on it. You may struggle with periods of doubt and deep introspection. Was the truth I was given as a child really true? Can I trust God's Word? Is Jesus really the one I should follow?

Let me encourage you with just a bit of counsel. First, periods of doubt and questioning are not uncommon. God can handle honest questions. So don't freak out and think that just because there are some questions cropping up in your mind that everything you've been taught as a child in church must be wrong. That is nonsense. Your faith can grow through times of questioning and even doubt to become stronger than ever before.

Secondly, just because someone raises questions that you can't answer doesn't mean the faith you have been given is flawed or untrue. You will be tested, but take time to think critically about every new idea and theory you hear. Listen to opposing ideas and opinions and make sure you keep a steady diet of spiritually vibrant and biblically sound teaching going on in your life. Stay active in a Bible teaching church and stay connected to spiritual mentors. When questions do rise, give godly people a chance to speak into the concerns you may have.

Yes, your faith will get tested and by some very smart people, but rest assured that people every bit as smart and learned as any professor you will ever hear have also wrestled with the same issues and concluded that the Bible is true and Jesus is Lord. Don't be thrown off by some smooth, sophisticated assault on your faith. The Christian faith has survived two thousand years and it has endured all kinds of assaults from intellectuals and skeptics. You do not need to fear the truth, just seek it. Long after the latest skeptic is gone and the latest fad has faded and the latest attack on your faith has been silenced, people will still find life and truth on the pages of God's Word.

You're going to have a challenging moment. You're going to have a gut check. I can promise you that. Just mark it down. You're going to have a moment in the next few years when you have to decide, "Do I really believe what I've been taught about God? Is His Word true or not?" It is what you decide in that moment that will make all the difference. So, before you go, remember what you've been taught.

Determine Whom You Will Follow

It is not only important to look back and remember what you have learned, but at this pivotal moment it is also important that you look forward to the Father you can trust. Remember what you've been taught and determine who you are going to follow. We cannot predict all that the future will hold. Tomorrow will have tests and challenges, mountains and valleys, days of sadness and days of joy. We can't know what tomorrow holds, but we can know who holds tomorrow. Follow Him.

Proverbs 3:5-6 are some of the most powerful and beloved verses in all the Bible and they form a fitting final word before you go.

> *Trust in the Lord with all your heart, and lean not on your own understanding; In all your ways acknowledge Him, and He shall direct your paths.* *(Proverbs 3:5-6)*

In Andy Stanley's wonderful book *The Principle of the Path,*[27] he reminds the reader of an ancient time when there were only four television stations from which to choose. I would add that during the same time, you also unimaginably had to physically get up and walk to the television to change a channel. Those were hard times and for some reason during those times, the powers that be had decreed that once a year everyone in America should watch the *Wizard of Oz*. Seriously. Once a year it would be broadcast and everyone would get excited about "Wizard of Oz Night." It was like Christmas, Easter, July 4th and "Wizard of Oz Night" were on the same list.

So during that yearly phenomenon our family would stay up to watch it. It was compelling cinema because the wicked witch was one creepy gal. I mean, to this day, a woman riding a bicycle kind of freaks me out. You know the story. Dorothy's at home and then there's a tornado. She and her dog, Toto, along with their house, get swept up into the tornado until it finally crashes in another land. Suddenly everything is in color. When she comes out of her crashed house, she sees that the wicked witch of the land was killed when her house landed on top of her. At this point the munchkins of Oz were all celebrating.

Then there was Glinda, the Good Witch of the East. She appeared wearing this huge dress. Dorothy, still very troubled even though she had landed on one of the bad witches, says to

Glinda the good witch, "I want to go home." Now the fact that that statement makes her the only adolescent in America or Oz who thought there was no place like home is irrelevant, but she wanted to go home. So Glinda, the Good Witch of the East, tells her that she must go to Oz and talk to the great Wizard, to which Dorothy asked the logical question, “How do I get there?” Glinda's answer: “Follow the yellow brick road.” Actually, it was, “Follow, follow, follow, follow, follow the yellow brick road.” So, all Dorothy had to do was follow the yellow brick road. Sure it took her through adventures and obstacles, and she picked up a few misfits along the way, but it was kind of simple. Stay on the yellow brick road and you’ll get where you want to go.

That really is what Proverbs has been saying all along. There is a path that will take you where you want to go and life isn’t so much about your circumstances as it is about your choices. Every choice is a course. Every decision is a direction. Every direction simply becomes a destination. All it takes is time. It would be nice if there was a yellow brick road I could show you today. Wouldn’t it be cool if I could say, “Hey, do you want a healthy family and a great marriage? Then follow the yellow brick road. Do you want to be financially sound, secure and free? Okay, just follow this yellow brick road. Do you want to overcome shame, guilt and bad habits? Just follow this road. Do you want to heal a broken relationship? Follow that road. It will take you right there”

That may sound overly simple, but the truth is that there really is a path. It’s not that easy, but there is a path. This path doesn’t just take you to a better life, it takes you to life itself. In fact, there is something better than just a path, there is also a person. The Bible says there is a person who will lead you right where you want to go.

In your early years you were given parents, mentors, teachers, pastors and coaches who tried to point you on the right path. "Walk here. Sit there. Do that," they said. But here's what every parent knows: we can't do that anymore. We're not supposed to. You're going to have to make your own decisions. You're going to have to make your own choices. We can't be there to say, "That's the path. Pick that one." However, there is a promise you can cling to. There is One who will always be there and knows the way. There is One who will never leave you. He will walk with you when no one else can. He will see you into the future He has planned for you and He will eventually see you home.

How can you claim this promise? How can you know God will direct your path? Just do exactly what Solomon advised,

Put Your Confidence in God

Trust in the Lord with all your heart. Put your full confidence in God. Know that God is there, that He is strong and that He is real. Put your trust in Him. Proverbs says,

> *...the fear of the Lord is a life-giving fountain. It offers escape from the snares of death.*
> *(Proverbs 14:27)*

Put God first in your life. Put your confidence in God. Trust in the Lord.

> *Blessed is the man who always fears the Lord, but he who hardens his heart falls into trouble.*
> *(Proverbs 28:14)*

Put your confidence in God. Believe in Him. Trust in Him. If you are reading this book and have never put your personal faith and trust in God, I pray you will do so now. God made you for His purpose and His plan. Each one of us has sinned and we stand guilty before God. We need forgiveness to make us whole and give us spiritual life. God loved us so much that He made a way by sending His own Son, Jesus, to die on a cross and pay the price of our sin and rebellion. When we acknowledge our sin, turn from it and place our trust in Jesus' sacrifice God will forgive us, come to live within us and give us the gift of true spiritual life: abundant on earth and eternal in heaven. If you have never made that choice, I pray that you will. Pray right now and ask God to forgive you, give Him control of your life. I encourage you to talk with someone right away who you know is a follower of Christ. Talk to them about your choice to trust Him and what you can do next to grow in Him.

If you have already made that decision, your choice today is to trust Him with your future and your life. Put your confidence in God, His Word, His will, His truth, and His power.

Put Human Wisdom in Perspective

Lean not on your own understanding. Solomon doesn't minimize the importance of human wisdom or human understanding. He spoke often about gaining wisdom. But here's what he said, "Don't lean on it." Don't build your life on what seems right. Don't lean on your own understanding. You need something bigger than your gut instinct. At some point, someone is going to say to you, "You just need to follow your gut" or "Follow you heart," but those are terrible ideas. Your instincts cannot be trusted. They will lead you to alcohol that can enslave you to an addiction, or to an immoral relationship that can ruin your life, or to a foolish financial decision that can put you in great bondage. Just because something seems right or feels right doesn't mean it is.

People follow their gut instincts into all kinds of turmoil and difficulty. Don't lean on your own understanding. Put human wisdom in perspective. The Bible says,

> *There is no wisdom, no insight, no plan that can succeed against the Lord.*
> *(Proverbs 21:30)*

That doesn't mean that there is no wisdom or understanding that you can gain from university professors, other coaches, pastors, or teachers. But it does mean that you should always put it in perspective. To the degree that it drives you to love God and build your life on Him, it's good and right, so learn all you can. On the other hand, to the degree that it leads you away from your foundation of truth, that's the degree to which you need to be careful. Consider human wisdom, consider your own understanding, but don't lean on it. Put human wisdom in perspective.

Accept God's Authority

In all your ways acknowledge Him. What does that mean? What does it mean to acknowledge someone? It means not only to recognize that they're there, but to listen to what they have to say. To acknowledge God's authority means to keep your focus on Him, to always be aware of His presence and to accept what he has to say as the final word.

To acknowledge God when you go off to college means that you should still be in church every weekend. That may sound simple, but if you're going to acknowledge God you need to pay attention to Him. A great first step is to get around some people who are studying the Bible and talking about God. In all your ways, acknowledge Him. Stay involved in church. Read your Bible. Acknowledge His presence on your college campus. Acknowledge His presence in that classroom. Act like God is on that date. In all your ways constantly remember that God is there. If you put your confidence in God, view human wisdom in perspective and acknowledge God's presence wherever you are, then this is His promise: *He will direct your paths.* He will take you and show you where to go. But that promise, which is as great as any promise in the Bible, is contingent upon you doing those three things. Put your confidence in God. Put human wisdom in perspective. Acknowledge Him in all your ways. Then God says, "I will show you where to go. I will direct your paths and they will be good."

Put Your Future in His Hands

What a comfort it is to know that you can put your future in His hands and claim the promise that the God of all creation will direct your paths. What a privilege to know that God will guide you through life. What will you study? What will your vocation be? Who will you marry? God has promised to direct your paths if you meet His conditions.

Do you remember Proverbs 4:18? My prayer is that this promise would be fulfilled in your life.

> *The path of the righteous is like the first gleam of dawn, shining ever brighter till the full light of day.*
> *(Proverbs 4:18)*

Perhaps for you, it's like the first gleam of dawn now. You have begun your journey. I pray you have found God and know Him through Christ. If so, you can see the light on the horizon just like the first ray of the rising sun. If you will walk in the paths of the righteous, God will guide and direct your every step, illuminating your path like the first light of morning that gets brighter and brighter and brighter.

In our role as parents, and now grandparents, my wife and I feel the power behind this verse,

> *My greatest joy is to know that my children walk in the truth.*
> *(3 John 1:4)*

It is our greatest joy and our deepest prayer. I pray that you will find the path, will follow the Father and will trust Him to lead you home. It's better than any yellow brick road and it will take you to a place far better than Oz. It will lead you into a place of God's greatest blessing.

Transitions are wonderfully hard. It can be difficult to turn the page, but what a comfort to know that when we can't walk every step with our kids anymore, there is one who can. When our youngest son, Stephen, graduated from high school, I pulled out on old poem that reminded me of the melancholy pains of letting go.

It's Tough on a Dog

It's tough on a dog when his boy grows up,
When he no longer romps and frolics like a pup.
It's tough on a dog when his boy gets old,
When they no longer cuddle on his bed when it's cold.
It's tough on a dog when his boy gets tall,
When he's off with the boys playing soccer and ball.
They no longer paddle through the mud and the bog,
Hoping to find a stray turtle or frog.
They no longer run through the grass up to their knees,
Or roll in the piles of fresh fallen leaves.

It's tough on a dog when his boy gets tall,
When he's off to the school, with girls in the hall.
It's tough on a dog when he has work to do,
And he forgets to play as he used to do.
It's tough on a dog when instead of the field or pond,
His boy becomes a man - and the man is gone.[28]

Before you close this book, I want to share with you one final letter that I wrote to my son. Maybe your parents will say something like this to you, or maybe not. What you must remember is that you have a heavenly Father who loves you more than any earthly parent can. The words of Proverbs aren't merely Solomon's words to the next generation, they are words from your Heavenly Father to you. Your Father wrote you a letter, it's the book of Proverbs, it's the entire Bible.

Maybe in this final letter you will hear the voice of your father, your mother or your grandparents. Maybe you will hear the voice of a coach, a mentor, or maybe just someone who loves you enough to point you to a heavenly father.

Dear son... Dear daughter...

And so it ends. And so it begins. I saw you take your first steps. Now I watch as you take the next step. It's a big one. You are ready, though sometimes I'm not sure if I am. I worry too much. I know the challenges you will face. I know the choices that will test you. We've tried to give you a foundation. We've tried to point the way. I'm sure I failed many times. Many times. But I hope somewhere along the way I said the things that really matter. I hope that somehow we have pointed you to the wisdom of God, to truth that can light your path. So before you walk out the door, there are just a few more things I want to say.

Tell the truth. Work hard. Care about people more than things. Character matters. Watch what you say. Be careful, but take a few risks now and then. Be courageous. Listen to those who are older and wiser. Never stop learning. Never stop dreaming. Laugh often. Love deeply. Love purely. Be slow to anger. Be quick to forgive. Make the most of every opportunity. Sing joyfully. Be a friend others would want to have. Give generously. Remember whose child you are. Remember those who have gone before and paved the way: teachers, grandparents, aunts and uncles, coaches, pastors. They believed in you, prayed for you, invested in you.

Most of all, remember God. He gave you life. He is the source of all wisdom. He will guide you even when I can't. He has a great plan for your life. Follow Him. Live for His glory. Only Jesus can forgive our sins. Only Jesus can make things right with God. Trust Jesus. Follow Jesus. Live for Jesus. I can't imagine anyone loving you more than I do, but I know that He saw you first and He holds you in His hand. My heart hurts to let you go, but I know He will never leave you or forsake you.

Love God with all your heart. Love others. No matter where life takes you, no matter what tomorrow holds, never forget I am proud of you. I love you more than words can say. The future belongs to God. It is a gift He gives to you. Seize it. Make the most of it. Don't look back with regrets. It is your time, and the time is now. Go. Live. Achieve. Dream. Work. Laugh. Endure. Believe. Hope. Love. This is your time, whatever you do and wherever the road takes you, always remember I love you.

END NOTES

Chapter One

1. The Poetry Foundation, *The Road Not Taken,* http://www.poetryfoundation.org/poem/173536.

Chapter Two

2. Chuck Colson, *Born Again* (Old Tappan, New Jersey: Fleming Revell Company, 1976), 208-224.

3. William Bennett, *The Book of Virtues* (New York: New York: Simon and Schuster, 1993), 605-606.

Chapter Three

4. James Merritt, *Friends, Foes, and Fools* (Nashville: Broadman and Holman, 1997), 37.

5. Colson, 104-105.

6. Stephen Covey, *The 7 Habits of Highly Effective People* (New York: New York: Simon and Shuster, 1989), 235.

Chapter Four

7. Vince Veneziani, *10 Lottery Winners Who Lost It All,* http://www.businessinsider.com/10-lottery-winners-who-lost-it-all-2010-5/ (May 6, 2010).
8. http://www.businessinsider.com/10-lottery-winners-who-lost-it-all-2010-5

9. http://www.businessinsider.com/10-lottery-winners-who-lost-it-all-2010-5

10. Ellen Goodstein, *Unlucky Lottery Winners Who Lost Their Money,* http://www.bankrate.com/brm/news/advice/20041108a1.asp/ (November 8, 2004).

11. http://www.businessinsider.com/10-lottery-winners-who-lost-it-all-2010-5

12. http://www.bankrate.com/brm/news/advice/20041108a1.asp/

13. http://www.bankrate.com/brm/news/advice/20041108a1.asp/

14. Susan Adams, *Why Winning Powerball Won't Make You Happy,* http://www.forbes.com/sites/susanadams/2012/11/28/why-winning-powerball-wont-make-you-happy/ (November 28, 2012).

15. James Dobson, *Love for a Lifetime* (Portland, Oregon: Multnomah Press, 1987), 70-71.

16. Charles Dickens, *A Christmas Carol*, (Philadelphia, Pennsylvania: The John C. Winston Company, 1939), 128.

Chapter Five

17. Friends, Foes & Fools, James Merritt, Nashville: Broadman & Holman, 1997.

18. Friends, Foes & Fools, James Merritt, Nashville: Broadman & Holman, 1997, p. 135

19. Merritt, 23.

Chapter Six

20. "How Pornography Works: It Hijacks the Male Brain," almohler.com, 10/9/2013

21. Religion in Four Dimensions, by Walter Kaufman: Published by Reader's Digest Press, Distributed by Thomas Crowell Co. New York, 1976, p. 311.

22. James Dobson, "Fatal Addiction," http://www.focusonthefamily.com/popups/media_player.aspx?MediaId=%7B710D67E8-7AFB-411F-8A37-503EA8B69B5B%7D.

Chapter 7

23. Forbes, *Thoughts on the Business of Life, http://thoughts.forbes.com/thoughts/work-theodore-roosevelt-extend-pity-to*

24. Robert Lupton, *Toxic Charity*, (New York, New York: Harper Collins, 2011), 6.

25. William Bennett, The Book of Virtues, New York: Simon & Schuster, 1993, pg. 347.

26. Finestquotes.com, *Excuses Quotes,* http://www.finestquotes.com/select_quote-category-Excuses-page-0.htm

Chapter Eight

27. Andy Stanley, *The Principle of the Path* (Nashville, Tennessee: Thomas Nelson, 2008), 9-11.

28. Jean Sawtell, as quoted in James Dobson, *Bringing up Boys* (Wheaton, Illinois: Tyndale House Publishers, 2001), 257.

CPSIA information can be obtained at www.ICGtesting.com
Printed in the USA
LVOW06s1150310314

379587LV00003B/4/P